The Rose Garden and the Ring

Faith in the Midst of Unfaithfulness

Lynn and Christine

WESTBOW
PRESS®
A DIVISION OF THOMAS NELSON
& ZONDERVAN

WestBow Press books may be ordered through booksellers or by contacting:

WestBow Press
A Division of Thomas Nelson & Zondervan
1663 Liberty Drive
Bloomington, IN 47403
www.westbowpress.com
1 (866) 928-1240

Because of the dynamic nature of the Internet, any web addresses or
links contained in this book may have changed since publication and
may no longer be valid. The views expressed in this work are solely those
of the author and do not necessarily reflect the views of the publisher,
and the publisher hereby disclaims any responsibility for them.

Any people depicted in stock imagery provided by Thinkstock are models,
and such images are being used for illustrative purposes only.
Certain stock imagery © Thinkstock.

ISBN: 978-1-4908-1144-4 (sc)
ISBN: 978-1-4908-1143-7 (e)

Library of Congress Control Number: 2013918577

Print information available on the last page.

WestBow Press rev. date: 8/31/2015

Dedication

This book is written for all those who have shared their stories and support for me during this time and belongs to all the Christian men and women whom are desperate for answers and hope. I dedicate this work to my children whose love and own faith has inspired me; and to my friends and family who have been a constant source of encouragement. Most importantly, to my God who showed me His promises are real.

—Lynn

———ᨋᨋᨋᨋᨋᨋᨋ———

I dedicate this book to my God who carries me, to my kids who walked through all of this with me and to my friends that have supported me. My hope is that this will help others the way you have helped me. Thank you for your endless love.

—Christine

Table of Contents

Foreword

Is the miracle you seek to breathe again? Do you find yourself inside a darkness you cannot escape? Are you broken in such a way that you have become like dust on the floor? If so, you are not alone. Lynn and Christine have been there. They have invited us into their secret places. Although two different stories, two different lives . . . you will discover they have the same God. A God of Healing and a God of Hope. That God is your God as well. These two women want to lead you to His throne through the power of scripture and the cries of prayers. You can trust them. They are real. They are honest. You will breathe again, darkness will turn to The Light, and ashes will turn to beauty. Just take their hands and be open to a God of Miracles.

See you at the throne,
A Sister Traveler

Preface

Two ordinary wives and mothers, living four houses apart, going about the business of family life suddenly discover their lives are connected more than they thought. A knock comes to Christine's door. There stands a child whose mommy is locked in her room and daddy is missing. It is so amazing how God pulls us together to give hope and encouragement to those who need it and to those who will need it! Christine had just been through what Lynn was about to endure . . . for the first time. Years later they find themselves faced with adultery for the second time, occurring within months of each other, hear Gods calling and begin writing a book, **The Rose Garden and the Ring**.

> *"But in my distress I cried out to the Lord; Yes, I prayed*
> *to my God for help. He heard me from his sanctuary;*
> *my cry to him reached his ears." (Psalm 18:6)*

Acknowledgments

First and foremost we give thanks to the Lord for choosing us to be a light. We acknowledge that without you we would not be where we are now. Thank you for placing us in each other's lives.

Special thank you goes to our initial editor and to our final editor. Your insight into the readability of this book was such a blessing. We appreciate your views, hard work, and time spent! We realize the sensitive nature of the topic and truly appreciate the thought and care you put into the corrections and advice.

For the Forward, we thank our dear friend. This was not an easy task and yet you put aside your emotions to help us in this endeavor.

Thank you to our children for agreeing to be a part of this ministry. We can't wait to see how God blesses you in the future.

Finally to our husbands, thank you for your financial and logistical support. You never stood in our way with our writing this past year. Special thanks to Christine's husband for organizing meeting locations for our work.

In Christ,
Lynn & Christine

Introduction

Dear friends, we are so excited to share **The Rose Garden and the Ring** with you! It is our story to tell and bring glory to God and a silver lining to our cloud. You will find that each chapter addresses a facet of our ordeal that can be read independently or from cover to cover.

We felt a calling to relay our experiences, faith, and friendship with others so that they know they are not alone. Our hope is to have people who identify with our situation, turn to their faith in God for answers, help, and healing.

"Hearing from both Lynn and Christine, this book not only opened my eyes to different perspectives, but also started me on my own journey of forgiveness toward my husband of 21-years, after his adultery and subsequent divorce. There are plenty of books out there about infidelity, but this is the first one I have read that allows for and voices the emotions that any spouse feels when going through this type of tragedy against families . . . and then puts you on a path of healing. These prayers, uttered by the authors, finally gave me my own prayers; words that I could not speak until I read theirs. Life-changing, heart-altering . . .
—Fellow Sojourner and Editor

Chapter 1

How 'BIG' is Your Faith?

"Now faith is confidence in what we hope for and assurance about what we do not see." (Hebrews 11:1)

Lynn's story . . . .

When I found an earring receipt in my husband's suitcase for earrings that were not for me, my heart sank and the once thought unimaginable began to become a possibility. I immediately phoned him and asked him about it and the only thing he had to say was, "we will talk when I get home," in a tone that was unfamiliar. That was not what I wanted to hear and as I pushed and pushed for an answer, he finally said that he was going to ask for a divorce the following week. This was coming from a man I had known for at least 15 years and was married to for twelve years, who told me he loved me often, called me several times a day on his work trips, was great with his kids, and didn't give me much reason to believe he had been unfaithful. We had two wonderful children ages six and eight. I became a stay-at-home mom years before, largely because he traveled for his job at least four or five days a week and we felt the kids needed stability. Fortunately his income was enough to make this situation possible. In a state of initial shock and disbelief, I began crying and praying. After hearing what little he had to say other than he wanted a divorce and after ensuring he left the house to stay wherever else, I came to the realization that evening that I had to make a very important decision right away.

I called myself a Christian and went to several Bible studies among other things over the past few years and I was now facing something huge, life changing, painful, and unimaginable. Was I going to just simply talk the talk or was I going to walk the walk? I chose to follow God's word and guidance instead of allowing my human nature to take over. That led to the start of a long and painful, yet rewarding journey, which resulted in my becoming closer to God than ever before, and to the return of a husband to his marriage and family.

<hr />

Christine's story:

I found a receipt for not one, but two necklaces. Both were gold rope chains. One was 16 inches and one was 18 inches and both were coupled with a charm. The two charms were a dolphin and a music note. I got the music note and only one necklace. My heart dropped into the pit of my stomach as I grasped on to the carpet beneath my knees and screamed. My entire world had just begun to spin out of control and I had no way to stop it! He came home to talk with me and proceeded to tell me that he was in love with her and had never truly been in love with me. We had two children ages two and four and had been together for twelve years, six dating and six married.

My husband showed no signs. He told me he loved me several times a day and called often throughout the day. He was very attentive and was attending and participating in church on a regular basis. We were doing so well. I had lost the weight from my second pregnancy and was getting back into shape while staying home with the kids and caring for the home. We were doing all of the things that are supposed to help keep a marriage together. I was always sure to find a sitter wherever we lived so that we had our date nights. Our kids went to bed at 7:30 every night so that we always had evening quiet time together. The only signs I had were those he had skillfully wormed his way out of. I think I would have believed anything not to have faced what was in front of me. I was a stay-at-home mom and I had forsaken all of my own dreams to follow my husband on his career track. This track took us out of our home state and to several different homes and cities. It was hard to say the very least.

He had been climbing the ladder at work for around eight years and seemed to have finally arrived. The job that we had aspired to and made sacrifices for was finally his. We were even able to move closer to home so we would be able to see our families more often. As if enough was not enough, we were offered another position even closer to home. So we began the search to relocate. After a brief search we found a cute home with, wait for it . . . , a white picket fence and a big backyard for the kids to play. We physically moved all of our things into the new home, but promptly learned that my husband had to return to the former city. The progress on the new office was not going as quickly as was planned and the old office needed a little more attention. They had prematurely moved us. What to do now? We lived in a hotel for about two weeks with daddy, but the kids soon drove me batty without room to run. We decided that it would be alright to have daddy stay in the hotel during the week and come home to us on weekends. So the kids and I moved in fully to our new home. And that is where our trouble began.

He became more of a workaholic than ever and I was very lonely. I did find a church to attend and got involved quickly so that I would have some adult interaction. This living situation was not unusual in his field of work, as he soon found out. I was lonely and I dove into church and hobbies, always waiting for his phone calls and the weekends. He would talk with his peers about how it was all going and dive right back into work. One day while chit chatting with a fellow team member, he received the level of empathy that he desired. My husband began to innocently talk with her about their similar work and living situations. They would check up on each other and eat together when they were in the same city. Then it became more. I do not know all of the details on how or why he allowed it to become this long affair, but it lasted for at least eight months. The relationship was one of the worst kinds. It was not just sexual or emotional, it was both. In fact, she once told me that they had even made wedding plans!

Needless to say, he began to pull away. The first signs were the missed evening phone calls to say goodnight to the kids and me. Then came the weekends where he was not able to come home. Finally, when he was home, he was so distant. He was always going out to make a phone call and the big one . . . he did not initiate sex.

The signs were all there I just didn't want to see them. I was so afraid and I missed him so terribly. We had been high school sweethearts, dating for six years and married six. He was all I knew and all I wanted. Panic set in. I began asking questions and eventually found the answer that I did not want to hear. He loved her and was leaving us. He said he had never loved me and that he felt sorry for me.

Face to the ground, I lifted the bottle of Goldschlager that a friend passing through had accidentally left at my house and I proceeded to pour a short glass. I was not a drinker, at all! My point in sharing this is simply to illustrate how "out of body" one can become at this crucial point. That one drink would probably do me in, so I called my father while on that floor, and said, "Daddy, I think you need to come and get me and the kids. My husband has had an affair and is leaving me. I am drinking and will not be able to drive to you." He immediately hung up and got to me in record time.

To say that I was desperate is an understatement. I was devastated in a way that is indescribable to anyone that has not been there. If there was one thing I knew and was as sure

4

of as the day is long, it was that I loved the Lord and that He was right there with me as I received the horrible news of my destroyed future. So now I had a decision to make. Do I stay or do I go? Better yet, does he stay or does he go? He was not interested in working it out, so I really had no choice but to cry out to my God for direction, and He alone was faithful. Throughout this journey that I was forced to face, I was not alone. I had the God of the Universe on my side and I was completely reliant on Him. I drew nearer and nearer to Him every day and formed a bond that was stronger than me. This is the journey we went on together, my God and I and we are still on it to this day.

If you are reading this, then you may have been where I've been. It is that overwhelming feeling that something is very wrong in your relationship or with your spouse. Sometimes the relationship has previously had its issues and yet for some, the marriage seems great, almost perfect or as perfect as two humans living under one roof can be.

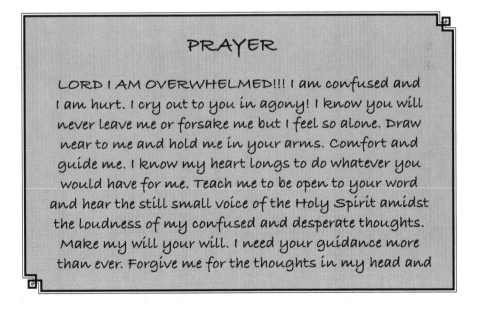

PRAYER

LORD I AM OVERWHELMED!!! I am confused and I am hurt. I cry out to you in agony! I know you will never leave me or forsake me but I feel so alone. Draw near to me and hold me in your arms. Comfort and guide me. I know my heart longs to do whatever you would have for me. Teach me to be open to your word and hear the still small voice of the Holy Spirit amidst the loudness of my confused and desperate thoughts. Make my will your will. I need your guidance more than ever. Forgive me for the thoughts in my head and the anger in my heart. Help me not to sin in my anger. I love you Lord and I want to follow the path you have set for me because I believe in your promises. AMEN

POWER

"My flesh and my heart may fail, but God is the strength of my heart and my portion forever." (Psalm 73:26)

Chapter 2

Walking with God

"Your own ears will hear him. Right behind you a voice will say, 'This is the way you should go,' whether to the right or to the left." (Isaiah 30:21)

When I said I walked with God I meant I prayed several times every day and night. I learned more about and practiced listening to the Holy Spirit so that I could be guided down the right path even if it didn't make any sense whatsoever! At the appropriate moment I was led to the verse, *"Trust in the Lord with all your heart and lean not on your own understanding; in all your ways acknowledge him, and he will make your paths straight."* (*Proverbs 3:5-6*). God didn't promise me that I would still have a marriage when everything was all said and done. He promised to make my paths straight IF I trusted in him alone. An individual from my Beth Moore Bible study who had been through a divorce but didn't trust in God or pray during her trial (but wished she had) told me to not focus on what my husband was doing or saying . . . only to focus on what God was doing and saying. That, my friends, is not as easy as it sounds! However, at specific moments when it truly appeared that he was a lost cause and our marriage was over, and after fervent prayers to God for incite, what I had thought to be true was entirely different. The good Lord gave me just enough information to keep me in the marriage, even if it meant only hanging on by a small, thin thread! I should probably convey right about now that when he left that first day he stayed elsewhere and finally ended up renting an apartment for six months.

It is important to mention that you must believe that God truly exists and can do anything. God gave us the Holy Spirit. If any of you have experienced what the Holy Spirit sounds like and feels like, it should be a welcome encounter. Jesus told us in his last days on earth that *"John baptized with water but in a few days you will be baptized with the Holy Spirit."* (Acts 1:5). *"The Counselor, the Holy Spirit, whom the Father will send in my name, will teach you all things and will remind you of everything I have said to you."* (John 14:26) Jesus taught us more about the Holy Spirit in the book of John. *"When he, the Spirit of truth, comes, he will guide you into all truth. He will not speak on his own; he will speak only what he hears, and he will tell you what is yet to come. He will bring glory to me by taking from what is mine and making it known to you."* (John 16:13-14). For me, during this time the guidance of the Holy Spirit was an overwhelming need to get on my knees and pray for whatever I needed to at that moment even if it did not make any sense. I couldn't even make it to the other room to pray . . . I HAD to pray immediately. At other times, the Holy Spirit guidance was an overwhelming feeling that something was not right and I felt that I had to pray continuously for anything and everything that came to mind.

———— ～ww∘o⦿∖e⟡⦿⟡⦾∘o∘ww ————

There are many ways to get from one place to another, as we all know. Vehicles, airplanes, boats, trains, cars and bikes all get us from point A to point B with minimal effort on our part, placing our faith in the one driving the mode of transportation. If we eliminate those vehicles, we are left with our own two feet. We still have options though! We can run, jog, hop, skip, jump or just plain walk. All but walking will get us there faster, but we might miss something along the way. Not to mention, it is hard to really spend time communicating with anyone else when we are doing anything besides walking.

All of that rambling to say I think *walking* with God is right where we needed to be at this time of our lives. In fact, as the poem about the footprints in the sand tells us, occasionally God has to reach over and pick us up and carry us. I know He has had to carry me, a lot! I am glad His back does not get tired easily.

When you walk with someone, you might chit-chat or discuss important topics, you may look around and see the beauty around you, you may even notice things that you have never noticed before. Often times when you are walking with someone you just walk quietly, enjoying the stroll and each other's company. That is where I would like you to consider starting, and if it gets too hard and you just can't go on, remember He is there to pick you up and carry you whenever you ask.

Go there in your mind for a moment. Imagine a quiet walk with the Lord, amidst all of the turmoil in your life. If you ask Him to come along side of you, He surely will. That is the first step. When I first talked to Him . . . wait, let me back up for a moment. If I am going to be honest with you, the first time I spoke with the Lord on this matter I did not walk or even talk. I jumped, yelled, screamed, cried and had a righteous fit about what I had discovered. So there, I suppose it would be the second time or so.

I began to pray like I had never prayed before. I spoke to Him while driving my car, taking a shower, making dinner, sweeping the floors; whatever I was doing, I was constantly in prayer. I prayed with a feverish desperation and I received answers. Whether from the mouth of a good friend or from the nudges of the Holy Spirit, I got my answers.

One story that really got me thinking and held my attention was the story I found in a book called *"How to Save Your*

Marriage Alone" but was actually right out of the word of God. Hosea.

The original retelling of the story of Hosea and Gomer is absolutely beautiful. I have included a short piece of the story below, but I truly hope you will take the time to look up the story in its entirety. Read the following and allow yourself a new perspective.

The Story speaks of a great love, born from an arrangement, and blossomed into a family. Hosea was a prophet of God to Israel, and a father of three. His wife, however, changed after the birth of her children. We pick up the story where Gomer has left the family . . .

The Love Story of Hosea

(Excerpts from a first-person dramatic sermon by Dr. John W. Reed, Associate Professor of Practical Theology, Dallas Theological Seminary.)

I found her (Gomer) in the ramshackle house of a lustful, dissolute Israelite. I begged her to return. She spurned all my pleadings.

I went to the market, bought food and clothes for Gomer. I would provide all her needs and she could think that they came from him. He struggled home under his load of provisions. I followed in the shadows.

She showered him with love. Her lover approached to embrace her, but she held him off. I heard her say, "No, surely the clothes and food and cosmetics are not from your hand but from the hand of Baal who gives all such things. I am resolved to express my gratitude to Baal by serving as a priestess at the high place."

I could not move. I saw her walk away. Gomer gave herself with reckless abandonment to the requirements of her role of priestess of Baal. She eagerly prostituted her body to the wanton will of the worshipers of the sordid deity.

Daily I prayed for Gomer and as I prayed love sang in my soul.

God moved me to go to Samaria. Soon I was standing in the slave market. Then I saw a priest of Baal lead a woman to the slave block. My heart stood still. A terrible sight she was to be sure, but it was Gomer. I wept.

Then softly the voice of God's love whispered to my heart. The bidding reached thirteen shekels, of silver before I fully understood God's purposes. "Fifteen shekels and an homer of barley." The bidding was done.

I paid him the price he asked. Then I tenderly and said to her, "Gomer, you are mine by the natural right of a husband." "I will restore you to the full joys of womanhood."

Reading in the Bible, you will see that sometimes God allows us out of a relationship in the case of marital unfaithfulness and sometimes He calls us to stay. That was a revelation to me. So many well intentioned people told me about how God allows us this one instance for divorce. They love us and mean well, but our walk with God is different in each situation. The story actually gave me comfort since I felt led to stay. I told myself, maybe I was not completely crazy, only mostly!

My decision was to walk through this with God at my side and if He wanted me free, He would make it so. I would do nothing to hinder or help, if at all possible. My days would be filled with my prayers, my children, and making myself all that I could be so that I would be prepared for anything God had for my future. Praise the Lord!

PRAYER

El Sali, God my Rock, Help me to remember to be in fervent prayer so I can hear you clearly. Teach me to recognize your voice. Help me to be still and quiet in your presence so that I do not miss a single word from you. Be my rock to lean on, to take a stand on your name, and to lift me closer to you so I can feel your presence. Walk with me through the darkness and light my path. Bathe me in the sunlight of your victories! Holy Spirit, remind me to continue the walk and pray without ceasing. Help me to pray for (spouse's name) so that his eyes are open to your truths even when I do not feel like praying for him. Let the thin thread that I am hanging on be woven into double braided rope, strengthened by your grace and mercy. Forgive me when my thoughts stray and when I feel like I cannot find you, for I know you are there, always. AMEN

POWER

"The Lord is not slow in keeping his promise, as some understand slowness. Instead he is patient with you, not wanting anyone to perish, but everyone to come to repentance." (2 Peter 3:9)

"But in my distress I cried out to the Lord; yes, I prayed to my God for help. He heard me from his sanctuary; my cry to Him reached His ears." (Psalm 18:6)

Chapter 3

Immediate Assistance/ Guidance

"Submit yourselves, then, to God. Resist the devil, and he will flee from you." (James 4:7)

Almost immediately after vowing to walk with God through my devastating situation, I felt like I needed to talk to a lawyer. My spouse was saying he wanted a divorce and I did not know anything about lawyers, the divorce process, or consequences of divorce. I did know it would benefit me and the children greatly to have my own lawyer instead of a joint one . . . whatever that meant. Yes, I know this might be construed as not trusting God but it was what I needed to do. I learned that it is not "giving up" or not "trusting" God or that I have no control by seeking a lawyer's advice but simply knowing what I could be facing someday. Once I was ready I called good friends for prospects. They immediately offered me assistance and within hours I had names and numbers and ultimately chose one with an excellent reputation who had served in the military, my former profession. I left a message for him and he returned my phone call that evening. He asked me my situation and mentioned that I needed to be sure the marriage was over because divorce was very serious and to give it a couple of weeks for things to settle. He did, however, answer all my questions and thus gave me a certain peace that I would be okay if worse came to worse. I had at least an idea logistically and financially of what I would be going through if that was to be my path.

As time went by other assistance/guidance made a much greater impact than a lawyer on getting me through the rough times. Those occurrences are listed in the next chapter entitled Tools and Weapons.

———∿∽⌒⊙⋆⊙⌒∾∿———

Let me begin by saying I know this is a long journey for you to be starting out on. It will be very difficult to feel sane at times. This is why my friend and I have decided to give you our stories and experiences. We are two very different women with similar situations, who deal with our stories in very different and similar ways. Did you get that? Maybe, maybe not; but I bet you think everything sounds ridiculous right now.

Reading this is the second thing you should do immediately. The first is to fervently pray. Pray for an open heart to hear what the Lord has for you through his word and through seeking advice from others. Pray that the Lord holds you in His arms and protects you from the attacks of the devil. And finally, pray for His guidance in reading this book. We know that it holds dear advice from hearts of love, compassion and empathy.

Now, let me restate that the first thing I turned to was not the Bible. I grabbed a bottle of liquor and called my daddy. However, the next day I was at the throne of the Almighty pleading for my sanity, for my marriage, for my kids and for my best friend. I am not ignorant in thinking that you can find out such a thing and say, "Hummmm, let me see what the Bible says about this." You are human, cut yourself a break and then get your priorities in order. You will have days that are good and days that are very, very bad. It is perfectly normal.

I also sought advice from an attorney. My father knew one that could advise me on the stance I had taken and how to protect myself and the kids. That was a very difficult appointment to go to. He told me that my state was a "no fault" state and it did not matter in the eyes of the court whether or not he was committing adultery. That was a stab I was not expecting. Then he proceeded to tell me that I was not eligible for alimony because we had only been married for six years; you had to have been married seven! Upon further discussion, my father, the attorney and I felt that a formal decree of separation was in order. The attorney drafted a document stating what the divorce papers would look like, but only in a separation. It was all very cold and legal, but it protected me and my kids from being left high and dry and secured my custody so the other woman could not take my kids from me. Again, I was not looking for a divorce, just some assurance, and that is just what I got. Just some assurance.

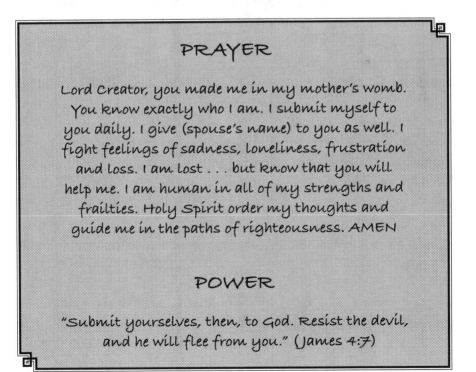

PRAYER

Lord Creator, you made me in my mother's womb. You know exactly who I am. I submit myself to you daily. I give (spouse's name) to you as well. I fight feelings of sadness, loneliness, frustration and loss. I am lost . . . but know that you will help me. I am human in all of my strengths and frailties. Holy Spirit order my thoughts and guide me in the paths of righteousness. AMEN

POWER

"Submit yourselves, then, to God. Resist the devil, and he will flee from you." (James 4:7)

Chapter 4

Tools and Weapons

*"He gives strength to the weary and increases
the power of the weak." (Isaiah 40:29)*

You are an emotional wreck from the moment you find out about the unfaithfulness and it only gets worse as you piece together the timeline of the affair and discover truths along the way. You will search for anything that will ease your pain . . . even if it is for only a moment. I am begging you not to turn to any unnecessary drugs or abuse of alcohol to try and forget the pain. Don't go after whatever is just a crutch and can cause more permanent damage. The following are some 'healthy' ideas that may work for you. Keep in mind that it will be unbearable and gut-wrenching many times but that it will lessen as your day's progress.

Counseling (friend)—Hopefully you are able to find a person who will listen to you at any time of the day. In all honesty, walking with God, learning new verses and trying to apply them can be overwhelming and confusing. Especially if you are trying to be "humble", "loving", "patient", in continuous "prayer", "listening" to the Holy Spirit, etc. all at one time! You need someone who can help you make sense of everything or at least help you be grounded again. I was fortunate enough to have a Christian friend in another state who knew my spouse and who would not judge either one of us. She felt led to help me by listening, at all hours, and praying for and with me. Be careful though whom you confide in because some people take everything too much to heart, feel helpless, and begin to stress themselves! Those friends should be on a need-to-know basis so they do not become weary. They can be there for you when you need other assistance, such as getting your children places or as just a friend you can be with to get away from things for a while!

Counseling (professional)—A couple of months into the separation my spouse informed me that we should go to counseling so that I couldn't ever say that he didn't try everything to make it work. Whatever. I insisted on a Christian counselor. My spouse said he was 99% sure that he wanted a divorce and told the counselor that as well so I had no idea what we were doing there. We went together and also separate for a while and had some good talks afterwards but his heart was not with God even though he was beginning to have doubts about ending the marriage. Apparently with the affair out in the open it was much harder and less exhilarating. I guess if the light shines on something dark you can see its true colors. At the early part of our marriage he went to accountability groups, Bible studies, church, and even taught Jr. High Bible study at our military base. So what happened? I think that the start of the downward spiral began when he changed jobs. All of a sudden he was away from us more than he was home due to work and in a Godless workplace around Godless people for the most part. I do recommend professional Christian counseling if you can afford it because after he said he wanted to come home he was fine, relieved the "drama" was over. Yeah for him. Unfortunately I was a disaster and needed counseling even more! Therefore I continued to go by myself for a time.

Books—You might discover that you will be trying to find any book, article, or pamphlet that deals with infidelity (like this one) so that you can make sense of things and be reassured that you are not the only one going through this. There are a few out there, but the one I turned to the most was the <u>Power of a</u>

<u>Praying Wife,</u> by Stormie Omartian. I have prayed the prayers in that book so much that I have some of them partially memorized!

Bible—Of course, if you are "walking with God" you will be opening the Bible many times to find answers. Joining a Bible study where there is homework is extremely beneficial! At my church during this time, we were studying Beth Moore's Bible study on the life of David. It seemed every lesson had what I needed to hear at that moment from God. So much so that one of my friends said she felt the lessons and videos were just for me even though the room was full of people! You probably will have topics pop up in your head from time to time and hopefully will open the Bible to see what God has say about it. Go for it! Learn! Build the relationship with God!

Music—Playing certain Christian songs over and over and over that touch my heart like "Praise You in This Storm" was comforting and enabled me to continue with the day. *See the *Playlist Suggestions* listed in the back of this book for more inspirational music.

Friends—Friends can help you get your mind off of things for a while and reassure you that you have value. True friends will sometimes not know what to say but just knowing they care helps tremendously.

Church/Prayer Chains—Letting people in on your private life can be embarrassing but when it comes to prayer there is strength in numbers. The bible says, "Though one may be overpowered, two can defend themselves. A cord of three strands is not quickly broken." (Ecclesiastes 4:12) Imagine what more than three people praying can do!

Prayer/Intercessory Prayer—God's word tells us to pray and to pray continuously! God's word tells us how to pray and what to pray for. I prayed on my face and sitting up with my hands together like on television at first but an interesting thing happened . . . instead of praying with my hands together and looking down I felt led to pray with my hands open and up, shoulder-width apart while looking up toward the heavens! I prayed in the car and around my home, by myself, with other people, and even with my children! I learned that I could also intercede for my husband in prayer. Praying for him, although not easy to do, helped soften my stance. I also noticed small changes in him.

Incidentally, praying for a person who is a Christian already and has invited the Holy Spirit into their heart is different from praying for a person who doesn't know Christ at all. If your spouse knows Christ then you could pray that God take the blinders off of his eyes to see the truth and to give him ears to hear His word. Otherwise you could pray for your spouse's salvation. You can tell God anything . . . He hears you . . . that's a promise!

———————

Holding it together on your own is too hard and is potentially dangerous. There are times when you just want to be alone, times when you want to be with others but say nothing, and other times when you want to emotionally vomit all over anyone who will stand for it. The dangers of depression and isolation are very real. Take courage, there are many places you can turn to for support.

- **A good counselor that is in line with your faith**—The first counselor was a Christian from a local church (not my own). He was nice and well learned, however, I left his office worse every time I saw him. I do not think it was his fault, we just did not mesh. Do not be afraid to admit if a counselor does not work for you. Seeing the wrong person just wastes precious time. The second was from a non-faith based counseling center. She had over 25 years of experience and a very gentle spirit. She made all the difference to me. I was able to speak and she just listened and guided. She was very affirming and open to whatever I had to say. That is how you need to feel when you leave the office.

- **This book ;)**—As we have stated before, we really hope this will make your journey a little easier, if there is such a thing.
- **The Bible**—*"For the word of God is alive and active. Sharper than any double-edged sword, it penetrates even to dividing soul and spirit, joints and marrow; it judges the thoughts and attitudes of the heart."* (Hebrews 4:12)

  There it is, right there. The Word penetrates. It is often able to reach you when no one else can. It is my comfort and my shield; when needed it is my sword of truth.
- **Edifying music . . . uplifting, or from a good time in your life**—I am a music person. So when I listened to the radio, whether Christian or secular, I could always twist the meaning of the song to apply to my situation. Then I would just get more depressed. I found that listening to music from a happier day does not seem to have the same affect. Call me crazy, but I can totally disassociate the song meaning and just enjoy the music if it is from a good time in my life.
- **Friends**—this is tricky. Some friends can handle it and some cannot. You have to determine that by their reaction upon telling them. Be careful not to drain a friend with negativity. Draw on their strength and encouragement. Beware of encouragement that guides you towards selfishness or vengeance. Now is not the time.
- **A pastor**—He is always there to listen and usually has a good bit of marital counseling under his belt.
- **Small group Bible study**—I relied heavily on my small group. There were women of all ages and backgrounds that were able to pour into my life. They prayed for me, listened to me and spoke words to me. The study we were in at the time was a welcome escape from my own head and into the heart of God.

- **Family**—All families are not created equal. At first my family did not know what to do. They were all in shock and were defensive for me. However, they tried to stay out of it. Then later they came alongside and supported me in whatever I needed. They were so good to me.

PRAYER

Lord! As hard as I try to keep order and peace in my home I feel like I'm just a train wreck! And the more I discover details about my spouse's deception, the more pain I feel in my heart even though I long for the truth. Holy Spirit, help me to use the resources that you bless me with and open my eyes and heart to your healing. I understand that I will probably not be rescued from the feelings of anguish but I'm pleading with you to point me toward the truth of the Bible and things you place in my life for comfort until this storm subsides and your glory is made known. Thank you for being my omnipresent (everywhere at all times), omniscient (all-knowing), and omnipotent (all-powerful) God. AMEN

POWER

"I love you, Lord; The Lord is my rock, my fortress, and my savior; my God is my rock, in whom I find protection. He is my shield, the power that saves me, and my place of safety." (Psalm 18:1-2)

"The weapons we fight with are not the weapons of the world. On the contrary, they have divine power to demolish strongholds." (2 Corinthians 10:4)

Chapter 5

Loss of Control/Power . . .

"Cast all your anxiety on him because he cares for you."
(1 Peter 5:7)

Fear of lack of control, of an uncertain future, of jumbled thoughts, and feelings of unanswered prayers can be overwhelming. Truth is . . . you can't control your spouse's actions and, in my opinion, stupid, unnecessary, hurtful, selfish, blind choices. So the most logical thing to do, and what the Bible suggests in many verses, is to give control over your situation to God. He wants us to trust in Him and He wants us to have enough faith in Him to know that He <u>will</u> take care of us.

I experienced many times when God's hand was at work and I knew it was God because I asked for an obvious sign. It would be something only God could have done. One time in my obsessive quest for details/information, an acquaintance called and said that she thought my spouse was on a dating website because HER friend came over and asked if she should send him a response message. She told me all that was on his web page and I said that yes, it was him. After I confronted him about the situation, he said that he had only signed up for the website three days prior and asked me how I could have possibly found out. During this period, however, we were supposedly seeing if our marriage could work and he was supposedly not seeing anyone. HA! It was just one of several events that I would have never known about without divine intervention.

But God's timing is not our timing. Many times I would give control to God and then take it back, attempting to manipulate situations, because I lacked patience. My spouse had to go through experiences in order to see clearly that the person whom he thought he was "in love" with was someone entirely different. In fact, he "broke things off" with her many times before finally realizing that the relationship built on lies was more of an infatuation fueled by the secrecy of it all. He even lied to her and went out with who knows how many other women! Speaking of lies . . . lying becomes a habit. Sometimes they lie to "not hurt our feelings." Other times their entire 'other' life was created from lies so it becomes normal for them. They even try to believe that their lies could be true, maybe, if "such and such". In other words, you will not be able to tell a lie from the truth most of the time because they get REALLY good at it. I don't know how that could not just be exhausting. (I could write an entire chapter with example after example of my spouse's lies).

So you see, you really do not have any control. There is no way you can predict your spouse's actions. Just give it up to God and when you take it back, give it up again and trust that your best interests are in His hands. You cannot change your spouse's mind or choices. It has to be his decision. Giving up control can only be done through constant prayer and can lead to a place of humbleness where He can work through you. Don't forget to pray! Pray for the Holy Spirit's guidance. Pray for answers. Cry out in prayer for whatever you want or need! God is listening.

———ᘯᓬᓬᘋᘙᓬ᙭ᘙᓬᘙᓬᘙᘙᓬᘋ———

The feeling of panic, the dread of the future and the decisions you must make, and the knowing that you really have no control over the outcome of any decision. These are all paralyzing feelings that come over you when faced with unfaithfulness. You feel you have no say in what is happening to you and/or your children and that your spouse holds all of the cards. For me, that was a hard emotion to conquer, because I am a control freak when it comes to my home and my children. I have always prided myself in having a happy and safe home. I plan evenings that will include the whole family so as to create a feeling of oneness in our home. We play like no one's business! I love to sing and dance and play games with my children, and yet, all of my laughter, fun, and even my dance was stripped away from me. It was even hard to allow myself to have fun because it felt so wrong in the midst of such destruction. How could I keep our family together? How could I continue this feeling of safety in the home? How could I keep my dignity and exude strength? How could I do anything but lie in bed and stare at the ceiling?

Is anything really worth the effort anymore? Does it matter to anyone that I try so hard and yet no one is hearing my cries for help? There is only one way to get beyond these feelings and that is clear. The only thing that will help you gain control over your emotions, family and marriage is to give up total control to the only one that can take control. Lay it all at the feet of Christ and He will give you rest.

I know that sounds easier said than done . . . and it is! But it is all you can do and all you need to do right now. The loss of control can be crippling in every aspect of your life. Being a doormat is not an option, although many days I was just that. Being super controlling and demanding will get you nowhere and even turn your spouse from you. (I did that too) There is no way to say with certainty how you will act from day to day; sometimes it seems like a cruel lottery of emotions just taunting you.

. . . Truth

*"You shall know the truth and the truth
shall make you free!" (John 8:32)*

Truth is a difficult word for me to sound out. I know that
the truth will make me free . . . but that is God's truth. I am
secure with His truths. It is earthly truths that baffle me. When
reeling from the aftereffects of a spouse's affair, truth seems
far away, cloudy, and unattainable. Consider for a moment
the laughable definition of the word *truth* . . .

Truth

1   a: archaic: fidelity, constancy
    b: sincerity in action, character, and utterance

2   a: the state of being the case: fact
    b: the body of real things, events, and facts: actuality

My feelings run amuck when I read this definition. First I
see the word *archaic* and I sarcastically smirk, then my smirk
becomes a resounding "Ha!" when I see fidelity as the next
word. There is nothing constant left in my life. The rest is just
sadly funny. Then I look at 2b and I read *the body of real
things, events, and facts* and I am done thinking it is laughable.
Now I am hurt and left wondering if I will ever have anything
resembling truth again.

I knew what I believed in spiritually, but I could not believe
in my marriage or commitment between a man and a woman
any more than I could change that definition above. I realized
that we had no truth. He did not tell the truth and truth did
not exist in this marriage. The only truth I could hang on to was
the Truth of God and His word and love for me. That is where I
filed my definition of truth for that time. I hope to be confident
in truth between a man and woman again one day. I do not
enjoy this feeling as I know no one does.

PRAYER

Psalm 23
The Lord is my shepherd, I shall not be in want.
He makes me lie down in green pastures,
he leads me beside still waters,
he restores my soul
He guides me in paths of righteousness
for his name's sake.
Even though I walk
through the valley of the shadow of death,
I will fear no evil,
for you are with me;
your rod and your staff,
they comfort me.
You prepare a table before me
in the presence of my enemies.
You anoint my head with oil;
my cup overflows.
Surely goodness and love will follow me
all the days of my life,
and I will dwell in the house of the Lord
forever. Amen

POWER

"Guide me in your truth and teach me, for
you are God my Savior, and my hope is
in you all day long." (Psalm 25:5)

"In your majesty ride forth victoriously in the
cause of truth, humility and justice; let your right
hand achieve awesome deeds." (Psalm 45:4)

"Never take your word of truth from my mouth, for I have put my hope in your laws." (Psalm 119:43)

"The Lord is near to all who call on him, to all who call on him in truth." (Psalm 145:18)

"Come to me, all you who are weary and burdened, and I will give you rest." (Matthew 11:28)

Chapter 6

Emotions . . . the Rollercoaster

"In my anguish I cried to the Lord, and he answered by setting me free." (Psalm 118:5)

It is good you don't know all of the details of the affair at the very beginning. When you do beg God for the truth, ensure that you are able to handle the pain that comes with it! Ask and you shall receive . . . in God's time. Be ready. Be in constant prayer. Be so humble that your strength can only come from God!

Unbearable pain, tears, sick to your stomach, stress, control, no control, tears, anger, desperation, sadness, tears, confidence, confusion, insecurity, tears. My initial reaction was a rollercoaster ride. If I didn't have children I would have been able to sit for hours and get nothing accomplished. My young daughter had made a comment once that she wanted a pool in the backyard and I could probably fill it with my tears! I had no desire to eat. Naturally, weight loss occurred, which is not such a bad thing in some cases, but the less you eat the less energy you have and the downward spiral continues until you do something about it! Sound familiar? I also continued to review thoughts such as:

— Why is this happening to me?
— What do I do?
— He can't really mean it!
— I don't know anything about divorce.

— My parents got a divorce and that is not for me!
— I don't know what to do or get done from day to day because I no longer have any focus or motivation!
— This isn't the person I married!
— Yes, I am free to get a divorce according to the Bible but God hates divorce and what if all this is happening to bring my spouse out of the dark and back into the light by uprooting and exposing all of the sins he currently treasures so we can have a pure and meaningful marriage in the end?
— This is probably the only way Satan can get to me and so is he using my spouse? If so I REFUSE to let him win! I say again, SOUND FAMILIAR?

God promises us peace. *"Do not be anxious about anything, but in everything, by prayer and petition, with thanksgiving, present your requests to God. And the peace of God, which transcends all understanding, will guard your hearts and minds in Christ Jesus."* (Philippians 4:6-7). After being led to this verse, I discovered that every single word or phrase in this verse needed to be dissected in order to get the complete meaning. For example, the verse says to not be anxious about ANYTHING. It doesn't say not to be anxious about this or that. It says to not be anxious about a darn thing. From experience this is truly hard to do consistently. We fall back on our human nature and think we can handle things and take over rather than completely trusting in God. The verse next states that in EVERYTHING, by prayer and petition WITH thanksgiving, present your requests to God. This is advice from Jesus. It is clear what and how we can find peace: *"Peace I leave with you; my peace I give you. I do not give to you as the world gives. Do not let your hearts be troubled and do not be afraid."*(John 4:27). I typed these verses, printed them out, hung them where I could see them and memorized them. Seek out verses that speak to you and do the same!

Jokingly, we call it our "Bipolar" days. I genuinely hope no one with the disease is offended, as it is just the nearest description we can think of to express in a single word how you honestly feel when going through this disaster. You are so emotional one minute, and absolutely cold the next. I was up then down, and sometimes I was just nowhere. It was like a rollercoaster of emotions. I often told my counselor that I am just trying to avoid the crazy in me. The loss of control, emotional ups and down and the future uncertainty was enough to drive anyone mad. As women and especially, I think, as women, we desire to have our "ducks in order". We meticulously plan out our days with our children to be sure they get the rest and nutrition they need, the education and play their development must have to grow, and the love they crave from day one. All of these things are running through our heads while we clean the house, do laundry, plan meals, work a job, and try to balance the many hats we must wear for the day. We are mothers, sisters, daughters, church members, employees, arm candy, devoted wives, and sex goddesses. The list could go on, but you get the picture. The balance for you is hard, but to throw in the curve ball of an affair, smashes every single hat you wear, making you not even want to play ball anymore.

Rest assured that the entire gamut of emotions is normal and acceptable. Your anger and frustration, fear and despair, loneliness and overwhelming sadness, your lack of care at times crippling you, is all a part of this process. Allowing those emotions while trying not to sin in those times, is what begins the process of healing. Masking those emotions is not an answer, nor is it at all productive. In all of the years that I have talked with women in this situation, I have seen many masks. Choose your vice:

Masking: in my definition feels like it only affects you. It is the more victimless and self-inflicted coping mechanism.

- Not eating
- Overeating

- Cutting
- Drinking
- Sleeping
- Self-indulgent behavior
- Shopping (Retail Therapy)
- Pain meds/drugs
- Busyness

Sinning: is more damaging to others as well as yourself. These things are truly harmful to others and are completely unfruitful.

- Revenge
- Finding my own affair
- Suicide
- And so on . . .

Not one of these things provides relief for more than a temporary moment. The pain will always be there. Eventually the pain will dull and the days will get easier. Avoiding it only delays the healing process and causes additional problems such as resentment and depression. Rest assured that I have used a couple of the above to escape for a brief moment. I do not condone it, but it is normal to want to turn to these. Just avoid sinning, or anything illegal or dangerous, for goodness sake. Instead we redirect your heart to the good tools you have acquired and start fresh.

You are important. You matter. You must take care of you right now. On a cruise ship, the attendants tell you to be sure to secure your own life vest before securing the vest of a child or person in your care. That is also true here. You must take care of you so that you make it through before you can even think about the kids, family or friends, or even your spouse, for that matter.

PRAYER

Elohe Mauzi, God our Strength, teach me to be humble in my speech and actions even though it doesn't seem fair that I am the one who needs to be humbled. Your word says that you guide "the humble in what is right and teach them your way." (Psalm 25:9) and you "crown the humble with victory." (Psalm 149:4) I release control of my future completely to you so that together we may be victorious and can shout to the world of your glory and goodness! Through my ups and downs help me to be respectful to those around me, keeping my emotions from affecting others. I love you Lord. AMEN

POWER

"Greater is he who is in you than he who is in the world." (1John 4:4)

He says, "I removed the burden from their shoulders; their hands were set free from the basket. In your distress you called and I rescued you, I answered you out of a thundercloud; I tested you at the waters of Meribah. Selah (Psalm 81:6-7)

Chapter 7

Views on Marriage/Divorce

As I began reading God's word on marriage, I noted some things. Malachi 2:15-16 says, *"Has not the Lord made them one? In flesh and spirit they are his. And why one? Because he was seeking godly offspring. So guard yourself in your spirit, and do not break faith with the wife of your youth. "I hate divorce," says the Lord God of Israel, "and I hate a man's covering himself with violence as well as with his garment," says the Lord Almighty."* Therefore, even though I felt released from the marriage in God's eyes because he had an adulterous relationship and I would be okay in the end, I felt as if I was not to go seek the divorce and file myself. He was not abusive. It was a matter between him and God. What if all of this was to uproot him from his sins by exposing everything, coming clean with all of it, so that he would be free to come back to the Lord? What if the way I reacted to the situation made all the difference in saving my husband? Satan couldn't get to me any other way because I was too strong and I was not going to let him win this one. Satan would be happy to break up all marriages for many reasons, such as children having to adapt to a broken family.

As earlier stated, I was fortunate enough to be in a Beth Moore Bible study at my church studying the life of David. It was as if David's life and struggles with adultery and with his faith along with the homework, videos and class discussions were counseling me almost on a daily basis, ensuring that I stay on

God's path and somewhat understand what was happening to me and to my husband.

———⁓⌁⌁⌁⌁⌁⌁⌁———

My perspective was that I had no perspective. I had never thought about divorce, and certainly not my own. As far back as I know, my family has never had a divorce. My parents were still married, and both of their parents and even my great grandparents were married until death. It was a foreign concept that only brought pain and devastation to friends I knew in high school. I remembered the girls bawling in the locker room and on the lunch patio. Divorce was awful and NOT a part of my life.

Fear gripped me with an unrelenting grasp. I knew nothing about the laws surrounding divorce and child custody. I did not know an attorney and I had no friends going through a divorce to ask questions. It was as if I had been dropped in a foreign country where everyone was speaking another language and I was just spinning in a dizzying, helpless circle. I needed advice and quick. I would not allow divorce unless God himself came down and told me I had His blessing. Although I really had no choice in the matter, seeing as my husband wanted a divorce, I knew in my heart that it was not for me. Through much prayer, it came to me that I had made a vow to God. I had not broken that vow, so why would I break it now. I did not want to go to heaven and have my heavenly father ask me why I gave up on my husband, and in essence, my God. I had no idea what His plan was for my marriage at that point, it all seemed so hopeless. However, I did know that the Word says that He hates divorce and I never wanted to do anything to disappoint Jesus. My vow was my vow. If my husband wanted a divorce, he would have to file on his own. I would never sign papers. I held to that decision all the way through the ordeal.

PRAYER

LORD, Creator, your word says in Matthew 19:6, "so they are no longer two but one. Therefore what God has joined together, let man not separate." I know how you feel about marriage and divorce. I know you have a perfect plan. Give me the strength, courage, and insight to follow your plan your way. However things may turn out in the end I know that you are with me and have my best interests in mind. Please keep me safe from the lies that Satan wants me to hear. I put my hope and my trust in you. AMEN

POWER

"Wait for the Lord; be strong and take heart and wait for the Lord."(Psalm 27:14)

"Greater is he who is in you than he who is in the world." (1John 4:4)

"He says, 'I removed the burden from their shoulders; their hands were set free from the basket. In your distress you called and I rescued you, I answered you out of a thundercloud; I tested you at the waters of Meribah.' Selah" (Psalm 81:6-7)

Chapter 8

Contemplating Staying . . . The Grass is Not Always Greener on the Other Side.

"But those who hope in the Lord will renew their strength. They will soar on wings like eagles; they will run and not grow weary, they will walk and not be faint." (Isaiah 40:31)

When my spouse returned he mentioned that the grass on the other side was greener because of all the extra manure (crap). Greener did not mean better. It took him months and months and months to realize that. I truly believe that they are blind or 'in the moment' or afraid of missing out on life so they covet other people's lives and relationships. But once their eyes are open to what the other person is like and what their life would truly be without you they figure out that the green is really brown. Unfortunately, sometimes it takes too long for them to realize this and they missed the opportunity for reconciliation!

Many times the guilty party will decide that they have messed things up pretty badly and determine that there is no hope for reconciliation so, they don't even bother trying. Not in the beginning, of course, because they are convinced they are doing what they need to do to be "happy". Happiness is a choice and Love is a decision.

Finances also play a big role in whether or not a marriage can survive. The hurt spouse, possibly being without much financial support but with children, will have to respond quickly to find a solution to money issues. There is no luxury of time and resentment towards the the spouse will build quickly for the additional hardships one must face! My husband had two things going for him . . . I was a Christian trying to listen to the Holy Spirit and he had a job that supported me and the children through this time. We were blessed that he was more than willing to make sure we were not on the street!

For me, I did not want a lying, cheating spouse but left the decision up to God. For my spouse, he had to come to his own decisions and choices. It took time and situations . . . <u>a lot</u> of time and situations.

―――――ᴡᴏᴏᴇᴛᴏᴏᴛᴏᴏᴍ―――――

I call it my "conflicted mood"; that blank stare into nothing that eventually ends in a sigh. My options were less than promising on both ends. It was not a win/win situation, but a lose/lose one, or that is how I felt. The Word promises in *1 Corinthians 10:13;* *"No temptation has overtaken you except what is common to mankind. And God is faithful; he will not let you be tempted beyond what you can bear. But when you are tempted, he will also provide a way out so that you can endure it."* The word tempted from the Greek language also means tested. So although I was not being tempted, I was being tested. My faith, my marriage, and my sanity were all in question. If I was to endure this, then I knew my God would surely deliver me safe on the other side. What side I would be on was the question. Should I try to save the marriage or would I be better off divorced?

Option #1 was to let him stay. I could not trust him anymore, and his mind was on another woman. He seemed to have no desire for our family. The work to restore a marriage with those odds seemed insurmountable. If he were to agree to give us a try, it would mean long hours of counseling, fighting, crying, questioning and pain. It would, with God's help, yield in a restored marriage.

Option #2, if he were to walk away, I would have the relief from the tension in the home. I could concentrate on myself and the kids. I could start over and find someone who wanted me for me and my family. My husband would move on and probably get remarried. Alright, that is fine for him . . . but I could not take the man I have loved all of those years being with another and being a stepmother to my children. The discomfort in this option was too much for me.

At the time and as far as I could see, the pain from option 1 was temporary and would end in possible happiness while the pain from option two was for life. The grass is no greener one way or the other. It is up to you to decide what you can and cannot handle. You are important!

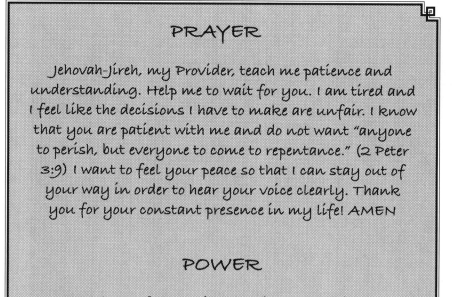

PRAYER

Jehovah-Jireh, my Provider, teach me patience and understanding. Help me to wait for you. I am tired and I feel like the decisions I have to make are unfair. I know that you are patient with me and do not want "anyone to perish, but everyone to come to repentance." (2 Peter 3:9) I want to feel your peace so that I can stay out of your way in order to hear your voice clearly. Thank you for your constant presence in my life! AMEN

POWER

"But do not forget this one thing, dear friends: With the Lord a day is like a thousand years, and a thousand years are like a day." (2 Peter 3:8)

Chapter 9

Our Sweet Children

"Her children arise and call her blessed; her husband also, and he praises her." (Proverbs 31:28)

Children truly do suffer when one parent leaves and wants to live another life. A person once said that children of divorce are changed forever and do not grow up to be the person they would have been. They can become stronger or stray as they grow from the experience. For some reason in which I will hopefully never understand, however, the person doing the fleeing doesn't always see it that way. They may have convinced themselves, or someone else has convinced them, that the children will be okay! That philosophy even comes from the mouths of those who were products of divorced parents themselves. My spouse said that he turned out pretty good.

My children were six and eight years of age and didn't understand everything but knew enough that a family unit is not supposed to be divided. They knew nothing of the affair but would find out eventually when they got older just like I did concerning my mother and her breaking up of the family. Growing up I became very quiet and withdrawn and couldn't wait to go off to college. My mom moved my soon-to-be stepfather into the house shortly after my dad moved out. My step-father was an alcoholic and every Tuesday and Saturday nights made our life miserable! That was the beginning of my withdrawal from everything. The marriage lasted only a couple of years but my life was forever changed. My middle school years were horrible. I do love my mom dearly, she took care of my sister and me as best she could, but to this day I do not forgive her. Maybe that is one reason why I was unable to write in the forgiveness section. I hope to someday learn how to forgive and be freed from bitterness.

The main priority became protecting the children from unnecessary information and putting them first when it came to spending time with their father. In spite of everything, my daughter began crying every day in her Kindergarten class for at least three hours per day, every day and wanting me to go with her to school. She once said she didn't want me leaving her like her daddy had and so it would be okay with her if I stayed in class all day. Fortunately we were blessed with a very understanding teacher who had been through something similar and would sometimes have to hold her in the rocking chair for hours while teaching. Both children eventually had to attend counseling at school. My son reacted in a more subtle way. He would pull his hood over his head in class and tear up or go into his room at home and close the door. He would stand facing his bed crying or simply make a statement in anger like, "when I grow up I will NEVER leave my family" and "I hate him." He obviously didn't hate his father but had a lot of anger. My daughter finally stopped crying in school when he decided to try and work on the marriage although still living in his apartment . . . a good thing because trust was definitely an issue. Even with this happening all around him, my husband still maintained that the kids would be fine. If a person is not listening to God then they are listening to Satan and I tell you what, he sure had my spouse convinced of quite a lot!

It is important to note that almost every time I mentioned what the kids said or did or felt he would get upset and respond that I was using them to make him feel bad enough to come back and being married just for the kids' sake wasn't a good thing.

As a result, I began to pick and choose what he knew and would mention it in the right context. People who have had affairs are looking for every reason to justify their actions and decisions, even when some are very aware of what the Bible says about adultery.

In spite of everything, I think my children were in much better shape than others going through the same thing because their father did see them often, taking them places and didn't introduce other people into their lives for the time being (as far as I know). Additionally, I tried to not talk badly about him to them but would consistently mention that he needed their prayers. As if tears from the situation itself weren't enough, listening to the beautiful, heartfelt prayer of a child could cause you even more heartache!

—————

My sweet babies! When I was a little girl, I would play house like many little girls. I would pretend to wake up, make breakfast, and kiss my husband goodbye as he drove off to work. I would care for the babies, do laundry, and tidy the house. Then my husband would come home from work and the babies and I would all be dressed in our best waiting for him. We would rush to the door to welcome him and then sit down for a lovely dinner. By that time, my real mommy was usually calling for me to clean up the mess I had made!

This is how I imagined raising children. This affair was not a part of my dreams for me, and certainly not for my baby dolls. The biggest part of the devastation sets in when you think of your kids and their futures. I never wanted this, I was completely out of control and my children were going with me. I suppose you could call me lucky in the respect that my husband was continuing to pay all of the bills, so the immediate financial worries were not a concern. However the future was in question. I had a four and two year old and no skills or college. There was no way I could provide without my husband's help.

He, like many other products of divorce, was under the impression that the kids would adjust and be fine. In fact, he felt like they would even be better off with two homes and families that loved them; a plethora of love! Ha! My family was not supposed to be this way; as I pounded my fists on the counter top. I became so very protective, to the point of denying my own feelings to protect theirs.

Don't you know I wanted to tell them exactly why their father would come to visit and then leave? I wanted to tell them just how bad he was and how he was the cause of their pain and not me. They would cry to me asking if they could call him, and when he would not answer, they would beg me to drive to him; which I could not do because he was with the other woman. He would miss scheduled visits with them and my little girl would sit on the door step in her best dress just waiting to see his car coming around the corner; and then the darkness would come. I would make her come inside and she would flail in my arms. Beating on my chest until exhausted from screaming, she would fall asleep. When he did finally keep a date with them, as he pulled away in his car, she would run down the middle of the street crying, "Daddy, don't go. Please! I'll be good. I promise!" over and over again. She would reach the end of the street and I would have to run after her, my own tears running down my face. I picked her up and she would beat on me crying that she hated me. I have never told him this.

These sweet babies do hurt. Whether or not we want to admit it, children do blame themselves on some level for the divorce/separation. They do want mom and dad together and happy. It makes them feel secure and safe. It provides an example for them of longevity, grace, mercy, and a 'never give up' spirit.

"Her children arise and call her blessed; her husband also, and he praises her." (Proverbs 31:28)

This is the desire of my heart and the hope for generations to follow. I want the best . . . the best, for my sweet children. With my Father in heaven, I will do all that I can to make that vision come true. The pain may be immense and even seem insurmountable. But, any goal worth reaching is attainable through faith, hard work and tremendous sacrifice.

PRAYER

Jehovah Raah, the Lord my Shepherd, you are the good shepherd. You laid down your life for the sheep of your pasture. You protect us from the wolf. You know me inside and out as I know you know my children inside and out. Lord guard my precious children's eyes, ears, and hearts from worry, pain, and negative influences. Guide me in caring for their needs. I lay my children at your feet. AMEN

POWER

"But from everlasting to everlasting the Lord's love is with those who fear him, and his righteousness with their children's children" (Psalm 103:17)

"Children's children are a crown to the aged, and parents are the pride of their children." (Proverbs 17:6)

"I am the good shepherd. The good shepherd lays down his life for the sheep. The hired hand is not the shepherd and does not own the sheep." (John 10:11-12a)

Chapter 10

Revenge

*"Be still before the LORD and wait patiently for him;
fret not yourself over the one who prospers in his way,
over the man who carries out evil devices! Refrain from
anger, and forsake wrath! Fret not yourself; it tends only
to evil. For the evildoers shall be cut off, but those who
wait for the LORD shall inherit the land." (Psalm 37:7-9)*

It is important to note that you should not seek revenge yourself. God promises that He will take care of that part and from experience, He does! You will try and help God figure out how to seek vengeance . . . car accident, getting beat up, loss of job and the list goes on. However, the best revenge is to do nothing except to sit back, pray continuously, and watch his appalling choices lead to terrible repercussions. One day I had to rescue him from a hotel because he had been beaten up the night before. He was defending his "friend". Some guys were talking about her being "easy" . . . hmmmm. His face was badly bruised and his nose and foot were definitely damaged. The amazing part was that his job takes him out of state every week but this incident occurred 40 minutes from home and so I was the one he needed to call for help! Another repercussion included losing a lot of his friends and distance from family members. They think that a separation or divorce is just between you and them. Not true . . . many of his friends felt like they lost him as well and were very hurt.

Some people think that revenge sex will make your spouse jealous but I have to tell you that it will just hurt you and unfortunately brings another person into the picture. At the beginning your spouse is 99.9% sure that your marriage won't work and really could care less what you do unless you sell his things. They just want to be free. They found someone else. Besides, you will want to remain without blame. It will make a difference to your spouse because he will notice the quality of person you really are compared to the adulteress he is seeing. You will want to be a person of good character, strong faith, and high values. You WILL stand out. My spouse always has said that he wishes that I would do something questionable so he could blame me for at least some of his decisions/choices. I would never give him that satisfaction!

———————

"Do not repay anyone evil for evil. Be careful to do what is right in the eyes of everyone. If it is possible, as far as it depends on you, live at peace with everyone. Do not take revenge, my dear friends, but leave room for God's wrath, for it is written: "It is mine to avenge; I will repay," says the Lord.

On the contrary: "If your enemy is hungry, feed him; if he is thirsty, give him something to drink. In doing this, you will heap burning coals on his head." Do not be overcome by evil, but overcome evil with good."
(Romans 12:17-21)

Attempt #1:

This is a tough chapter to write. There are just so many things I could say . . . where to begin. OK, maybe I will come back to this chapter another day.

Attempt #2:

Tonight I am remembering all of the ideas of revenge that I had all those years ago, and I am thankful that the Lord held me back. It must have been a divine force because I had some well thought out plans:

- Pour sugar into the gas tank of his beloved project car, because it meant more to him than I did.
- Keep the kids from him
- Tell everyone I know how horrible he is
- Tell his boss so he will lose his beloved job, or at least get in big trouble
- Tell his best friend so that he would abandon him and be ashamed of him
- Tell HER husband and family
- Beat the living daylights out of her
- Beat the living daylights out of him
- Take all of the money from our accounts and hide it from him

All of these and more came to mind on a daily basis. When I told his best friend, he did not hate him! He felt compassion and I looked silly. One time I actually jumped through the driver's side window of our car over my estranged husband and to the passenger side seat right at "her" neck. I grabbed her scrawny neck with every intention to hurt her, not kill her; just hurt her. The emotion came from seeing her with him in our car driving side by side. It was just too much and I cracked. Unfortunately, the outburst only made me look like a fool because no one knew why I had such hate for her. They had no idea about the affair and just thought I had lost my marbles. It was not pretty and I accomplished nothing. It was horrible to say the least.

Thank God His mercies are new every morning!

Attempt #3:

"Do not take revenge, my dear friends, but leave room for God's wrath." (Romans 12:19)

"Do not seek revenge or bear a grudge against anyone among your people, but love your neighbor as yourself. I am the Lord." (Leviticus 19:18)

"Another dies in bitterness of soul, never having enjoyed anything good." (Job 21:25)

"Each heart knows its own bitterness and no one else can share its joy."(Proverbs 14:10)

"Get rid of all bitterness, rage and anger, brawling and slander, along with every form of malice." (Ephesians 4:31)

Today, I hope to turn over a new leaf in this chapter. I received my inspiration for the day through a movie, of all places. Movies usually upset me these days. This one encouraged *living,* no matter your circumstances. I began to search the Word for an answer to revenge in response to the movie. My search began with the word "revenge" and ended with "bitterness". As I went deeper into the scripture, I realized that bitterness is what drives my hatred and desire for vengeance. I know that it is the Lord's job alone to deal in justice and revenge, but the bitterness in me took over and clouded my thoughts. I am not saying that I will never wish I could take some form of my anger out on one or both of them, but my eyes are open to the reality that I cannot. After all, how big is my God? He can see ways to help me deal with this and feel vindicated much bigger and better than I can. I will leave it to Him.

Bitterness cannot take over my heart. I want to live. I want to live for my Lord. I want to live for my kids. And I want to live for ME. I want to enjoy life, however my life may look in the future and I cannot do that harboring all of this anger and bitterness. Today I choose to embrace my life and that which Christ has in mind for me. I will go outside and smell the fresh air, take a walk, and be me. My kids will benefit from it and my husband will notice the change. I am taking control of this one tiny aspect of my life. Yes, I know I will fall from time to time, but today is precious and I will not waste it! Thank you Lord for fresh insight!

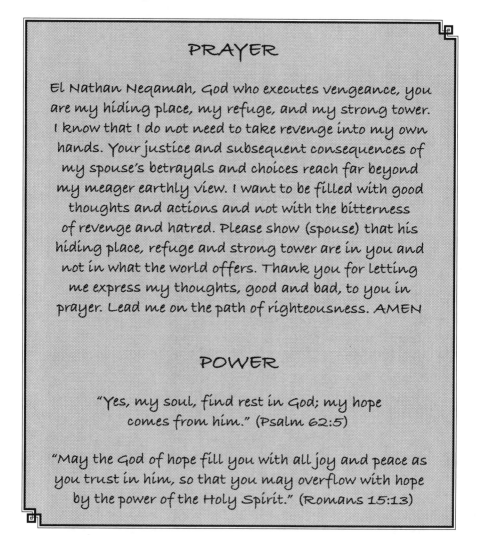

PRAYER

El Nathan Neqamah, God who executes vengeance, you are my hiding place, my refuge, and my strong tower. I know that I do not need to take revenge into my own hands. Your justice and subsequent consequences of my spouse's betrayals and choices reach far beyond my meager earthly view. I want to be filled with good thoughts and actions and not with the bitterness of revenge and hatred. Please show (spouse) that his hiding place, refuge and strong tower are in you and not in what the world offers. Thank you for letting me express my thoughts, good and bad, to you in prayer. Lead me on the path of righteousness. AMEN

POWER

"Yes, my soul, find rest in God; my hope comes from him." (Psalm 62:5)

"May the God of hope fill you with all joy and peace as you trust in him, so that you may overflow with hope by the power of the Holy Spirit." (Romans 15:13)

"Know also that wisdom is like honey for you:
If you find it, there is a future hope for you, and
your hope will not be cut off." (Proverbs 24:14)

"Do not repay evil with evil or insult with insult,
but with blessing, because to this you were called so
that you may inherit a blessing." (1 Peter 3:9)

Chapter 11

Open Your Eyes to God's Blessings "Amidst the Storm"

"When the storm has swept by, the wicked are gone, but the righteous stand firm forever." (Proverbs 10:25)

After reading scripture over and over for years, and especially during this time, I thought that if I was faithful, listened to the Holy Spirit, and tried to do what the scripture suggested, then at the end of my trial I would receive nothing but blessing after blessing. However, I discovered that the blessings were coming in the middle of the "storm" even before my trial was over and I needed to open my eyes and recognize them as such! Your spouse will probably not recognize the blessings because he is still deep into whatever he has gotten himself into. So you might be wasting your breath trying to tell him/her about them . . . or maybe not?! Incidentally, a little bit after I found out about the infidelity my friend gave me a journal and suggested I write down thoughts, feelings and events as often as I could. It was a great idea and it's a good way to not miss what God is showing you.

God never leaves you during this time and gives you glimmers of hope to keep you going. There will be little and big things that will happen that will be answers to prayers but not necessarily what you actually prayed for. It will be obvious to you that those "things" will be from God if you remain in prayer continuously. Therefore, remain in prayer daily! That sounds easy but sometimes you will want a break from prayer and that is okay too. There were times when I just asked God to comfort me through the night and take care of everything else because I just needed a good night's sleep. The Lord says, *"In the same way, the Spirit helps us in our weakness. We do not know what we ought to pray for, but the Spirit himself intercedes for us through wordless groans."* (Romans 8:26)

————꩜————

His blessings were seldom as evident in my life as they were during this time. It was almost comical how obvious God was at times and how He used these blessings to my benefit in ways that I could not even see at the time. One time, I needed my lawn mowed and a young man from church heard me tell a friend that I could not get my mower started. He offered to come and mow my yard until my husband returned. Now that young man happened to be way too young for me to ever consider a relationship with. I say that because he took his shirt off while mowing (and he was in great physical shape). All that to say that I was just so blessed that he would do that for a woman at his church, and I knew God had provided. What I didn't know was at the exact time he was mowing; my husband drove by to spy on me! He was shocked at his jealousy, so my husband retaliated by re-landscaping the entire yard while I was gone one day! God has a sense of humor even when his children are hurting. I was given a used washer, when mine was broken. People stopped by and called just when I needed it. The list goes on and on. The storm was raging, but God took care of me all the way.

The biggest blessing was my unexpected pregnancy. Yes, I said it! Not to get into too many details, suffice it to say that one night, I let him stay at my house. I felt the Holy Spirit allowing and even encouraging it. Two weeks later I was vomiting. I took a test. It was positive. Now of course, I had my cry over it, but only because of him, not the baby. At that point, I knew I had to take care of myself and this new life in me. I began to cheer up and focus on me, rather than the pain of separation. That beautiful new life saved me in so many ways.

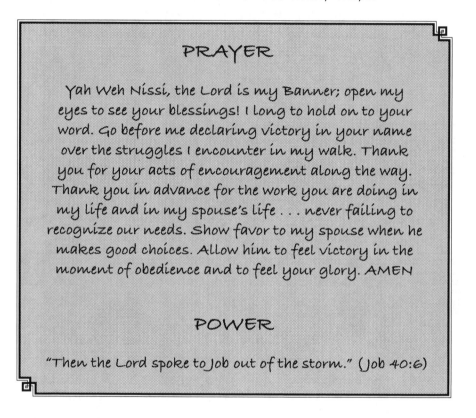

PRAYER

Yah Weh Nissi, the Lord is my Banner; open my eyes to see your blessings! I long to hold on to your word. Go before me declaring victory in your name over the struggles I encounter in my walk. Thank you for your acts of encouragement along the way. Thank you in advance for the work you are doing in my life and in my spouse's life . . . never failing to recognize our needs. Show favor to my spouse when he makes good choices. Allow him to feel victory in the moment of obedience and to feel your glory. AMEN

POWER

"Then the Lord spoke to Job out of the storm." (Job 40:6)

Chapter 12

Anatomy of an Adulteress

Carefully, we tread on this topic. We realize that not every woman who falls into adultery is exactly this woman depicted in the scripture. However, this is the Word of God and we make no excuses for it. We do not judge. We are simply hoping the faithful spouse will gain what is needed to guard the marriage. It is so important that she set herself aside as the wife God has made her to be.

"For <u>the lips of the adulterous woman drip honey,</u>
and her speech <u>is smoother than oil;</u>
but in the end she is **bitter as gall,**
sharp as a double-edged sword.
Her feet go down to **death;**
her **steps lead straight to the grave.**
She **gives no thought** to the way of life;
her **paths wander aimlessly,** but she **does not know it.**

Now then, my sons, listen to me;
do not turn aside from what I say.
Keep to a path far from her,
do not go near the door of her house,
lest you lose your honor to others
and your dignity to one who is cruel,
lest strangers feast on your wealth

and your toil enrich the house of another.
At the end of your life you will groan,
when your flesh and body are spent"
(Proverbs 5:3-11)

[LOVE IT!!! Can the Bible be any clearer? The adulteress should be avoided . . . DUH! There is so much more in the Bible about adultery . . .]

Warning Against Adultery

"For this command is a lamp,
this teaching is a light,
and correction and instruction
are the way to life,
keeping you from your neighbor's wife,
*from the smooth talk of a **wayward** woman.*

*Do not **lust** in your heart after her beauty*
or let her captivate you with her eyes.

For a prostitute can be had for a loaf of bread,
*but **another man's wife preys on your very life.***
Can a man scoop fire into his lap
without his clothes being burned?"
(Proverbs 6:23-27)

[Go God! You tell us Lord!]

Warning Against the Adulterous Woman

"My son, keep my words
and store up my commands within you.
Keep my commands and you will live;
guard my teachings as the apple of your eye.
Bind them on your fingers;
write them on the tablet of your heart.

Say to wisdom, "You are my sister,"
and to insight, "You are my relative."
They will keep you from the adulterous woman,
from the wayward woman with <u>her seductive words</u>.

At the window of my house
I looked down through the lattice.
I saw among the simple,
I noticed among the young men,
a youth who had no sense.
He was going down the street near her corner,
walking along in the direction of her house
at twilight, as the day was fading,
as the dark of night set in.

Then out came a woman to meet him,
<u>dressed like a prostitute</u> and with crafty intent.
*(She is **unruly and defiant**,*
*her feet **never stay** at home;*
now in the street, now in the squares,
*at every corner **she lurks**.)*
She took hold of him and kissed him
and with <u>a brazen face</u> she said:

"<u>Today I fulfilled my vows,</u>
and I have food from my fellowship offering at home.
So I came out to meet you;
<u>I looked for you</u> and have found you!
I have covered my bed
with colored linens from Egypt.
I have perfumed my bed
with myrrh, aloes and cinnamon.
Come, let's <u>drink deeply</u> of love till morning;
<u>let's enjoy ourselves</u> with love!
My husband is not at home;
he has gone on a long journey.

He took his purse filled with money
and will not be home till full moon."

With <u>persuasive words</u> she <u>led him</u> astray;
she seduced him with her smooth talk.
All at once he followed her
like an ox going to the slaughter,
like a deer stepping into a noose
till an arrow pierces his liver,
like a bird darting into a snare,
*little knowing it will **cost him his life**.*

Now then, my sons, listen to me;
pay attention to what I say.
Do not let your heart turn to her ways
*or **stray** into her paths.*
***Many are the victims** she has brought down;*
*her **slain** are a mighty throng.*
Her house is a highway to the grave,
leading down to the chambers of death"
(Proverbs 7)

I think we get the idea that being the adulteress is not good thing. However I do not want to discount the part of the other person. I am sure my husband initiated encounters. He definitely kept the relationship going and lied many times. He is not blameless and pure . . . but he can come to Godly repentance and be forgiven if he so chooses as can she.

When it came to the "other" person or persons, the book <u>His Needs, Her Needs</u> addresses some interesting ideas. Every person has certain basic needs. "In most affairs he or she meets only 1 or 2 of the basic needs. The betrayed spouse still fulfills 3 or 4." For example the adulteress might fulfill the need for sex (exciting because it's different and secret); communication (their taste in music may be the same); and admiration (she is in "awe" of his status and achievements and just preys on his insecurities).

But the betrayed spouse still has the need for family commitment (spending valuable time as a family); feeling safe and secure; feeling that the kids are taken care of (they don't feel as guilty); honesty (they don't have to worry about being deceived); love/sex (not infatuation or lust but unconditional love); appearances (he doesn't look like the bad guy); communication/history (no-one can replace 20 years of experiences together, memories, life before kids). The kind of needs the adulteress meets when the situation comes to light changes and becomes boring. What would be the result if you took away most of the needs you provide? (You still have to take care of the kids ☺)

———— ∿∿⋅∘⊙∿∘⊙⊙⋆∘⊙∘∿∿ ————

WOW! This is a hard one to write on. I have such negative thoughts concerning "her". Forgiveness by God's will and not my own is required here. But, let's get right into the anatomy, or make-up of the other woman.

Above, I have included the major verses in the Bible dealing with her. In my dissection of the scripture, I came up with the below. The <u>underlined</u> words are the <u>"attractive"</u> words concerning the anatomy of the adulteress. This is about as far as a man's mind and body allow him to see. In fact, the Word says that even she herself is unaware at times (no excuse). It is who she is. Her lips drip honey; her speech is smoother than oil (remember that oil is not easy to wash off); she is beautiful and she captivates with her eyes; her words are seductive; she dresses like a prostitute; and has crafty intents. She claims to have fulfilled her vows to her husband, and comes looking just for your man making offers of deep drinks of love-making laced with pure enjoyment. She leads with persuasive words and her face is brazen . . . stop right there. I had to look 'brazen' up because I had no idea what the true meaning of that word was. *It means marked by insolence and bold disrespect; the synonyms for brazen include audacious, bold, brash, brassbound, brassy, cheeky, cocksure, cocky, fresh, impertinent, impudent, insolent, sassy, saucy, and wise.*

Now, if you have a firm grip on what that says, gasp with me at the words in bold disrespect, audacious, cocksure, insolent, sassy and saucy . . . and WISE. All of these words are true and coupled with her cunning "wise" ways, we have a real adversary! She is confident in her shameless disrespect and good at it. She is also luring men with her clothing, body language and words. OUCH! That is all I can say to that; (not really, I can always say more).

I am amazed that God calls her out with all of these adjectives. It helps me to know what I am up against so that I can determine what I want to be, how I want men to see me, and what adjectives I want people to use when describing me.

Take a moment and know that I KNOW that I am different. Despite all of my faults and failings, I seek the Lord on a regular basis and He walks with me every step. However, let me just state for the record . . . . My lips <u>do</u> drip with honey. That is a similarity (hehe). I do not wander aimlessly. I have a plan to benefit those I love and bring glory to God through my life. I order my home. My number one priority (after God) is my husband and my children. That said, I am careful to care for myself so that I am pleasing to my husband as well as my personal standards. "Happy Mommy: Happy Family"!

Conversely, we have to discuss the words in **bold**, these are the words that describe the **real her** after she has gotten what she wants. The Word *promises* that she will turn bitter and sharp as a double-edged sword, with her feet leading to death and the grave. She wanders aimlessly with no thought for morality, and she may not even realize it. This wayward woman preys on his very life offering pure lust. Unruly and defiant, she never stays at home, but rather goes lurking in the streets for her next victim. (Sounds like . . . hmmmm . . . can you say Satan?)

I do believe the Bible does an ample job of telling us just what she looks like. Rest assured, ladies, that we are nothing like her. Do not get trapped in the all too familiar snare of comparison. Rather, purpose yourself to contrast her, setting yourself aside for the glory of God and as a trophy of pride and joy to your husband. The attractiveness you have is much more valuable whether physical, emotional, moral or spiritual. The Lord will reveal your beauty when He is able to peel the blinders off your spouse's eyes, whether it is too late or not. You will be restored, in Jesus name!

PRAYER

Elohay Mishpat, God of justice, I am finding it very difficult to pray. On my own it is impossible for me to understand and forgive. In time, teach me how to forgive her and my spouse for the pain they have caused me, my family and my friends. I thank you for your promises made clear in your Word. And as much as I am able, I give the adulteress to you; I trust you. Keep me from taking it upon myself to handle. Restore me as a child of God, not a person of this world. AMEN

POWER

"Charm is deceptive, and beauty is fleeting; but a woman who fears the Lord is to be praised. Honor her for all that her hands have done, and let her works bring her praise at the city gate." (Proverbs 31:30-31)

Chapter 13

God's Promises

"Commit yourself to the Lord whatever you do and your plans will succeed." (Proverbs 16:3)

Time and perseverance . . . You must go through the process and not be rescued from the emotional ups and downs until it is time or you will miss what God has for you to learn. God desires to bless us and to help us grow us spiritually. Diving into His word and recognizing His promises gives us comfort, direction, and a goal. He desires to make each of us an example of His glory and pass that heritage down to future generations.

God promises abundant blessings if we meet with Him daily, pray fervently, meditate on His word, and share with others. It is never too late to begin walking a God-driven path of righteousness. It is okay to stumble and fall along that path as long as we pick ourselves up, dust ourselves off, and keep moving forward. Lord knows we have had to pick ourselves and each other off of the floor MANY times along the way.

There are so many blessings in the Bible that it would be impossible to list them all. Together we have chosen some of the verses and organized them into manageable and familiar subtopics that we feel are applicable to our lives at this time. We welcome you to read and dwell on the following scriptures:

Destroy the Power of the Enemy

"God blesses those who are kind to the poor and helpless.
He helps them out of their own troubles. He protects
them and keeps them alive; he publicly honors them and
destroys the power of their enemies." (Psalm 41:1-2)

"If you return to the Almighty, you will be blessed again.
So remove evil from your house." (Job 22:23 NCV)

"Blessed is the man who always fears the Lord but he who
hardens his heart falls into trouble." (Proverbs 28:14)

Blessings

"Blessed is the man who perseveres under trial, because
when he has stood the test, he will receive the crown of life
that God has promised to those who love him." (James 1:12)

"But even if you should suffer for what is
right, you are blessed." (1 Peter 3:14a)

"If you are insulted because of the name of
Christ, you are blessed, for the Spirit of glory
and of God rests on you." (1 Peter 4:14)

Grace

"From the fullness of his grace we have all received
one blessing after another." (John 1:16)

"The Lord longs to be gracious to you; he rises to show
you compassion. For the Lord is a God of justice. Blessed
are all who wait for him!" (Isaiah 30:18)

Fellowship

"I will enjoy blessing them. With all my heart and soul I will faithfully plant them in this land." (Jeremiah 32:41 GW)

"I'm eager to encourage you in your faith, but I also want to be encouraged by yours. In this way, each of us will be a blessing to the other." (Romans 1:12 NLT)

"It is more blessed to give than to receive." (Acts 20:35)

"Blessed is the man who finds wisdom and gains understanding." (Proverbs 3:13)

Financial

"A generous man will himself be blessed, for he shares his food with the poor." (Proverbs 22:9)

"A faithful man will be richly blessed, but one eager to get rich will not go unpunished." (Proverbs 28:20)

"People curse the man who hoards grain, but blessing crowns him who is willing to sell." (Proverbs 11:26)

"Bring the whole tithe into the storehouse, that there may be food in my house. 'Test me in this,' says the Lord Almighty, 'and see if I will not throw open the floodgates of heaven and pour out so much blessing that you will not have room enough for it.'" (Malachi 3:10)

Material Blessings

"All these blessings will come on you and accompany you if you obey the Lord your God: You will be blessed in the city and blessed in the country. The fruit of your womb will be blessed, and the crops of your land and the young of your livestock—the calves of your herds and the lambs of your flocks. Your basket and your kneading trough will be blessed. You will be blessed when you come in and blessed when you go out. The Lord will grant that the enemies who rise up against you will be defeated before you. They will come at you from one direction but flee from you in seven. The Lord will send a blessing on your barns and on everything you put your hand to. The Lord your God will bless you in the land he is giving you." (Deuteronomy 28:2-8 NLT)

"I will cause my people and their homes around my holy hill to be a blessing. And I will send showers, showers of blessings, which will come just when they are needed." (Ezekiel 34:26 NLT)

"The Lord blessed Job in the second half of his life even more than in the first half of his life." (Job 42:12)

Protection

"Lord, you have stored up great blessings for those who honor you. You do much for those who come to you for protection, blessing them before the watching world." (Psalm 31:19 NLT)

"Blessed is he who has regard for the weak; the Lord delivers him in times of trouble. The Lord will protect him and preserve his life; he will bless him in the land and not surrender him to the desire of his foes." (Psalm 41:1-2)

"The Lord's curse is on the house of the wicked, but he blesses the home of the righteous." (Proverbs 3:33)

Generations

"After Abraham's death, God poured out rich
blessings on Isaac." (Genesis 25:11 NLT)

"For those who are always generous and lend freely,
their children will be blessed." (Psalm 37:26)

"Blessed is the man who fears the Lord, who finds great
delight in his commands. His children will be mighty in the
land; the generation of the upright will be blessed. Wealth
and riches are in his house, and his righteousness endures
forever. Even in darkness light dawns for the upright, for the
gracious and compassionate and righteous man. Good will
comes to him who is generous and lends freely, who conducts
his affairs with justice. Surely he will never be shaken; a
righteous man will be remembered forever. He will have
no fear of bad news; his heart is steadfast, trusting in the
Lord. His heart is secure, he will have no fear; in the end he
will look in triumph on his foes. He has scattered abroad
his gifts to the poor, his righteousness endures forever;
his horn will be lifted high in honor." (Psalm 112:1-9)

"The memory of the righteous will be
a blessing." (Proverbs 10:7)

Daily Faithfulness

"Jesus said, 'Blessed are those who have not seen
me and yet have believed.'" (John 20:29)

"Blessed is the man who trusts in you." (Psalm 84:12)

"I pray that your partnership with us in the faith may be
effective in deepening your understanding of every good
thing we share for the sake of Christ." (Philemon 1:6)

"The one who plants and the one who waters have one purpose, and they will each be rewarded according to their own labor." (1 Corinthians. 3:8)

"Blessed is the one who does not walk in step with the wicked or stand in the way that sinners take or sit in the company of mockers." (Psalm 1:1)

"Do not repay evil with evil or insult with insult, but with blessing, because to this you were called so that you may inherit a blessing." (1 Peter 3:9)

"Blessed is the man who makes the Lord his trust, who does not look to the proud, to those who turn aside to false gods." (Psalm 40:4)

"Blessed are all who fear the Lord, who walk in his ways." (Psalm 128:1)

"Blessed is the man who trusts in the Lord, whose confidence is in him." (Jeremiah 17:7)

"He who pursues righteousness and love finds life, prosperity and honor." (Proverbs 21:21)

From the Word

"Blessed are those who hear the word of God and obey it." (Luke 11:28)

"Even more blessed are all who hear the word of God and put it into practice." (Luke 11:28 NLT)

"The man who looks intently into the perfect law that gives freedom, and continues to do this, not forgetting what he has heard, but doing it—he will be blessed in what he does." (James 1:25)

"Blessed is the man . . . whose delight is in the law of the Lord, and on is word he meditates day and night. He is like a tree planted by streams of water, which yields its fruit in season and whose leaf does not wither. Whatever he does prospers." (Psalm 1:1-3)

"Do not turn aside from any of the commands I give you today, to the right or to the left, following other gods and serving them." (Deuteronomy 28:14)

"Whoever gives heed to instruction prospers, and blessed is he who trusts in the Lord." (Proverbs 16:20)

Praise

"Praise be to the God and Father of our Lord Jesus Christ, who has blessed us in the heavenly realms with every spiritual blessing in Christ." (Ephesians 1:3)

"Blessed are the poor in spirit, for theirs
is the kingdom of heaven.
Blessed are those who mourn, for they will be comforted.
Blessed are the meek, for they will inherit the earth.
Blessed are those who hunger and thirst for
righteousness, for they will be filled.
Blessed are the merciful, for they will be shown mercy.
Blessed are the pure in heart, for they will see God.
Blessed are the peacemakers, for they
will be called sons of God.
Blessed are those who are persecuted because of
righteousness, for theirs is the kingdom of heaven.
Blessed are you when people insult you, persecute you and
falsely say all kinds of evil against you because of me."
(Matthew 5:3-11)

"Now that you know these things, you will be blessed if you do them." (John 13:17)

PRAYER

El-elyon, the most high God, I praise you for your word, instruction, and blessings. Your promises encourage me to move through and beyond my current struggles. I ask you to continue to remind me to turn to your word when I fall. Use me and bless me! Amen

POWER

"But those who hope in the Lord will renew their strength. They will soar on wings like eagles; they will run and not grow weary, they will walk and not be faint." (Isaiah 40:31)

"I can do all things through Christ who strengthens me." (Phillipians 4:13)

"Now to him who is able to do immeasurably more than all we ask or imagine according to his power that is at work with us." (Ephesians 3:20)

Chapter 14

Understanding What He Is Going Through

"But a man who commits adultery lacks judgment; whoever does so destroys himself." (Proverb 6:32)

I have to admit that I don't really know what it is like to cheat. I never thought I would have to deal with mine and my children's broken spirits. I didn't care about what he was going through. I hoped he suffered greatly, and if possible, suffered more than I did because of his actions and of what we had to go through. At times I did notice anguish in his face and he gained weight but he was still blind and careless and so I wanted HIS distress to continue.

I can imagine at this point he is: panicked, overwhelmed with guilt from hurting everyone close to him; ashamed from the loss of respect he once had; and grief/pain from losing precious friends and finding not a lot of comfort from new acquaintances. I do need to mention at this point that the Bible speaks of the differences between earthly repentance, the kind in which you are sorry for hurting people and Godly repentance, in which you are truly repentant and make changes in your life to avoid further wrongs. It is important to distinguish the two.

However—yes I know you are thinking "here it comes"—one does need to address the "why he strayed" issue. Temptations are everywhere. Porn is easily accessed these days through many forms of communication (commercials with women in their underwear on public channels seriously?! Geez I have a son also!) Sexting, Skype, and infidelity (stemming from simple flirtations) are all commonplace and almost accepted in today's society. Pride, position of power, need for approval, alcohol, drugs (prescription and recreational), other influences, tempting situations, and the need for guy time are just a few more examples.

My husband has a job that is highly respected and is in a position of power. He travels approximately five days out of a week which in and of itself is a recipe for disaster. Especially harmful if the person is an atheist or weak in their faith. A person has to be strong to avoid the temptations and not give in to them. It seems as though several men are just weak. For example, a man will most likely not leave his wife and family unless he has somewhere else to go and someone else to be with. It seems as though he needs to be secure in the other relationship before making any moves toward leaving. This can be true for women as well.

Maybe it is a good thing that I will never understand his choices. I just need to look toward heaven and be an example. The Lord says:

"No temptation has seized you except what is common to man. And God is faithful; he will not let you be tempted beyond what you can bear. But when you are tempted, he will also provide a way out so that you can stand up under it." (1 Corinthians 10:13)

"But since sexual immorality is occurring, each man should have sexual relations with his own wife, and each woman with her own husband." (1 Corinthians 7:2)

For me, understanding him is easy and hard at the same time. You see, my spouse is in a position of authority wherever he goes. He is 'head' of the family, a leader in church, prominent in his sport, and in a very powerful position at work. Pride comes before the fall, for sure! *"Pride goes before destruction, a haughty spirit before a fall."* (Proverbs 16:18) Every time he has fallen, I have seen the surge of pride in him build up and build up to overflowing. He thinks he can fix it all, do it all, and handle it all. Humility is a far concept in these times. I can honestly say that he is an overall humble person when his pride is in check. He is constantly reminded of his very humble beginnings and his blessings.

My spouse's issue stems from the addiction to acceptance and a hero complex, I believe. (Not an excuse!) As a boss, a leader and a prominent figure, he is expected to show care for others; and don't you know the vixens of this world latch right on to that care. These women begin to mistake his concern and chivalry for attraction. So they take that and run with it. It begins with eye contact, subtle flirting, etc . . . until he is what he calls "accidentally" in a situation he did not see coming. Now, I do not excuse him. He made a choice. Studies have shown that men do know where the line is and when they are crossing it. My husband continued to make that choice by entertaining the idea and acting on it. Lying to me came next and then a total denial of right and wrong. Finally, he tried to justify his actions. The slippery slope is just that, slippery. There are no ropes or tree branches to hang on to when you begin in this downward plunge.

Rest assured, as I made very clear in the chapter on the adulteress, how plotted and planned, cunning and wise she is. The man does not know or see this initially, and if he does, it is a normal part of his history, so he thinks nothing of it. They deny and deny until they fall. This fall is complex in and of itself. I do not write this in sympathy of him, but in wisdom from unfortunate learning. The "fallen person" is not sleeping, not eating, unable to concentrate, and possibly suffering from medical issues. If he says he is "fine" or "happy this way", he is most likely covering up. He is so busy convincing himself that he is alright, that he actually begins to believe it. That is unfortunate and ends up hurting everyone. Truth is best, and lies only complicate.

My situation may not be the same as yours, but I knew my husband was suffering, even before he was caught and finally admitted to his infidelity. He was shut off from me, working more than necessary and keeping extremely busy. He was not asking for intimacy and that alone was a warning sign! Something was very wrong with him and I could tell. However, he was "in love" with "her", and because he knew he had done the unthinkable, he decided to keep that relationship going. He never imagined that I would be able to forgive him, so he decided to drive me away with cruel words.

**Additional Account: A dear friend shared an interesting story about her husband's confession. He was caught on pornographic websites by his young son and subsequently his wife. After the confrontation, the truth was disclosed and he took to his knees praying Psalm 139: 23-24. "Search me, Oh God, and know my heart; test me and know my anxious thoughts. See if there is any offensive way in me, and lead me in the way everlasting."

For two weeks he fervently prayed those verses, wrestling with the truths he did not want to confess. After the two weeks of prayer it was revealed to him that in order for him to grow in Christ he would have to tell his wife of the long term affair he had five years prior. After everything was out in the open the healing could begin. The accountability to his family and godly men in the church were the keys to his rebuilding of his faith and marriage. The marriage survived and is a success story. However, the struggles and temptations continue to exist but how they deal with them makes all the difference. Each spouse needs a personal relationship with God that is their own and God should be at the center of their marriage.

PRAYER

Johovah Ori, the Lord my Light, I intercede in prayer for my spouse and the temptations he faces. I pray that you open his eyes to see the light of your truths and ward off the evil of this world. Make him deaf to the negative influences and attune to your words and your way so that he is able to rise above. Take captive his heart and cause him to be a man after your spirit. Lord, if he says "hear my voice when I call Oh Lord; be merciful to me" (Psalm 27:7) I know you will be there to answer his plea. Let his pride be in his wife and children, his walk to be toward you, his sleep to be instructional (Psalm 16:7), and his awake time to be fully aware of your plans for him. AMEN!!!!!

POWER

"And you must show mercy to those whose faith is wavering." (Jude 1:22)

"Search me, God, and know my heart; test me and know my anxious thoughts. See if there is any offensive way in me, and lead me in the way everlasting." (Psalm 139: 23-24)

"But a man who commits adultery has no sense; whoever does so destroys himself." (Proverbs 6:32)

"Many are the plans in a person's heart, but it is the Lord's purpose that prevails." (Proverbs 19:21)

"For since the creation of the world God's invisible qualities-his eternal power and divine nature-have been clearly seen, being understood from what has been made, so that people are without excuse." (Romans 1:20)

"There is only cursing, lying and murder, stealing and adultery; they break all bounds, and bloodshed follows bloodshed." (Hosea 4:2)

"But I tell you that anyone who looks at a woman lustfully has already committed adultery with her in his heart." (Matthew 5:28)

"My son, keep your father's command and do not forsake your mother's teaching. Bind them always on your heart; fasten them around your neck. When you walk, they will guide you; when you sleep, they will watch over you; when you awake, they will speak to you. For this command is a lamp, this teaching is a light, and correction and instruction are the way to life, keeping you from your neighbor's wife, from the smooth talk of a wayward woman." (Proverbs 6:20-24)

Chapter 15

The Final Days

"The Lord is not slow in keeping his promise, as some understand slowness. He is patient with you, not wanting anyone to perish, but everyone to come to repentance." (2 Peter 3:9)

Pride and humility seem to go hand in hand. Pride will keep your spouse from coming back home because he doesn't want to tell everyone that he was wrong. Additionally, pride will keep you from wanting him to come back because he did you wrong and what would people think?

Months later I told a neighbor down the street that he had moved out. Our children played together all of the time but we were too busy to really know what was going on in each other's lives. It turned out that she had the same thing happen to her. She remained faithful to the course she felt God had shown her which resulted in her husband returning to God and his family. She immediately provided me with what helped her make it through and said she would pray for us daily. (As a side note, your spouse returning is not a given. No matter how faithful you are in your walk your spouse makes his own choices. Each of us, however, will be better off following the path God has set out for us regardless of reconciliation.)

A month prior to my husband returning home, my neighbor she said she had a message for me. Just like Jesus died on the cross for our sins even though he was blameless and pure, was I willing to humble myself, strip away all of my pride, to save my husband? She had to be kidding! Could I get ANY more humble? The answer was "yes." That night something happened that brought me to my knees once again in tears and prayers. I was a strong, independent person so to break me completely would be tough. It was the third event, in a series of three that made me humble and I needed my spouse's help. The second was my car, my only means of transportation, was crashed into while parked outside my home. I suddenly needed help getting the kids places and repairing the car. My independence was limited for a while. The third event occurred just 10 minutes after he left the house for his apartment. I started to take a shower and looked in the window at a real life 'peeping Tom'. Now, the only place, my home, that I felt secure and comfortable in, had been violated. I no longer felt safe and called the neighbors and the police. I actually needed my spouse once again so he had to come back and stay. I was truly humbled after that breach of safety, definitely feeling vulnerable. It softened my heart and showed my spouse that he still had a place in our home and family.

It wasn't fair that Jesus had to die and it isn't fair that I should suffer so much so that my husband could be freed when he deserved NOTHING from me! But Jesus did die for OUR sins and rose again for our salvation, *"For God so loved the world that he gave his one and only Son, that whoever believes in him shall not perish but have eternal life. For God did not send his Son into the world to condemn the world, but to save the world through him."* (John 3:16-17). Was I willing to sacrifice my pride and feel even sharper, stabbing, unbearable pain for my husband's salvation and to save my marriage?!?! Think on this question . . . are YOU willing to sacrifice your pride?

The last days before my spouse AND Christine's spouse returned to their families, even though years apart, had something in common. By this time we had basically written the marriage off and were barely speaking to our spouses. She was pregnant and had to take care of herself and her other two kids. I had to take care of myself and my two children as well. I felt like all my attention for the last eight months was spent on worrying, stressing, obsessing, praying and trying to work things out and basically ignoring everyone else only to be crushed over and over again. I quite frankly had no love left for anyone.

One day, he wanted to "talk", same as Christine's husband years earlier. They started asking questions and made statements like "How can you forgive me after what I've done to you?" and "It would almost be impossible to save our marriage." Surprisingly, although not really, our answers reflected God's word and promises such as the verses; *"Then Peter came to Jesus and asked, "Lord, how many times shall I forgive my brother when he sins against me? Up to seven times?" "Jesus answered, "I tell you, not seven times, but seventy-seven times." (Matthew 18:21-2); "For nothing is impossible with God." (Luke 1:37)* When Jesus was tempted by Satan in the desert in the book of Matthew he responded with God's word and at the end Satan left.

The questions and statements kept coming. All the advice given to him by the adulteress and other misguided "friends" he had made during his rebellion came up. All the "truths" he thought he knew and was starting to wonder about came to light. I know the following supposed "truths" sound familiar; the kids will be fine; you deserve someone who loves you; I want you to be happy. These statements are made by them to help them justify their actions and try and relieve guilt. I know for sure that the adulteress said them to him because I read the email! Remember, you are blameless and hopefully have remained blameless (i.e., left the revenge to God.) After our conversation he left, acting tough and in control but really totally confused. I, of course, was still bitter, exhausted, and "over it." So I had hoped and thought . . .

Seven days later I received an email from a Bible chain I was a part of, not knowing the author personally, that quoted the verse *"It shall come to pass that before they call I will answer and while they are still speaking I will hear." (Isaiah 65:24)* I had of course been fervently praying. She also wrote that she tried to send her message but when it came time to send it the text disappeared. The leader tried to find it many times but couldn't. The leader felt that someone needed to hear this and would try to find it and resend it in the morning. She found it, sent it and I received the message. It read that she was reminded of the time in Daniel when he prayed and the answer was sent the day he prayed but delayed 21 days due to a spiritual battle. (Daniel 10:12-13) She also wrote to "whomever needed to hear this that God does hear . . . He does answer . . . and to keep praying because there could be a spiritual battle going on keeping you from hearing His answer." Also, it mentioned that Daniel was told to "set your heart to understand, and to humble yourself before your God, your words were heard." That night I jumped on the emotional rollercoaster again and prayed and cried for six hours for God to just give me a direction and the peace that goes with it! I needed to know if I was to hold on because He was working on my spouse's heart or let go to move forward without him and divorce was inevitable because he was hopeless. I was definitely at the end spiritually and emotionally. The next morning, looking horrible from getting very little sleep, I had to chaperone my son's field trip. It was on the field trip that I thought I knew the answer. I was to let him go completely and plan for a future without him. And so I began thinking about what to do next to achieve that goal. I hoped to get some peaceful rest as soon as I could before making any decisions.

He came to get the kids that afternoon for a while and asked if I wanted to talk. I said "no" because I really didn't have much to say but he insisted. So we talked. I mean <u>he</u> finally talked. It was as if I was listening to God speak to me through him, answering my prayer for a clear direction. My spouse said he was tired of rebelling and wanted to commit 100% to the marriage and move back in the next day. He said he called "her" and ended the relationship for good and wanted to start appreciating me for the awesome person I was and was sorry for hurting me. He spoke in clear, to-the-point sentences, for the first time out of left field and there was no doubt it was from my God who knew I truly needed a direction. I have looked back often at that time wondering if he was supposed to return and that is the thing about God . . . he makes things happen so that it could only be from divine intervention. I will never doubt that the outcome was from God. I had my direction. Funny how I assumed the opposite! The resolution came eight days after the questions and a new beginning was starting. How was that going to work???

———— ᴡᴏᴏᴏᴏᴏᴏᴏᴏᴏᴡᴡ ————

The final days of your struggle will be unknown. There was no huge warning sign for me. I just went to a place of deeper prayer, if that was possible. I began to pray for the lies he was telling and for the truths to be revealed. I prayed for his heart to be turned back to mine. One day he told me that he was going out of town over the weekend to a car show. Somehow I knew that was not where he was going, but even more important, I knew that he needed to NOT GO to wherever or whomever he was going to. I began to pray for God's intervention. I asked God to stop him, in the name of Jesus, from going if that was in line with His will. I prayed, accepting whatever consequences this prayer would bring; sickness, a problem at work, accident, whatever! Boy did God show off for me! As he was driving down the highway while closer to my home than hers, his car "threw a rod" rendering the car done, finished, the end! His car was his first love and his heart was broken. In his distress, he called for me to come and get him! Why me? He had wanted nothing to do with me for so long! God was able to turn his heart. He had to stay the night on my couch. That night reminded him of the comforts of home and family.

Realizing Mother's Day was approaching, his wheels began to turn. He knew our kids were too small to do anything, and he wanted to one up the cute boy that had just mowed my lawn. (EGO) I was sure he would forget or spend it with "her", so I decided to go be with my mother this year. I left the house early that morning so I would not have time to be disappointed by my husband's lack of action. The day was beautiful. My parents had wrapped a gift for my children to give to me! I came home late that night, just before the kid's bedtime. What I found at my home was the beginning of his transformation, and mine.

I pulled up to the house to find a very dirty, tired and dehydrated husband standing in my driveway. His eyes lit up like they had not in months when he saw me pull up. He was excited like a child and very nervous to show me what he had done for me. I was less than receptive, thinking he did not deserve praise for anything! That was not important though. God had broken him right there in my yard that day. You see, he did not have a key to my house, so he could not come in for rest and relief from the heat. He had just spent the whole day re-landscaping my entire yard! In the dirt that day, he said to himself "Christine is going to LOVE this." Baffling himself he wondered why he even cared what I thought, and the love he had for God, for me and for the children began to flood his heart. From that night on, he began to make plans to come home. I had no idea he was planning to reconcile, but he began the process all on his own.

If that was not enough, that very weekend, my husband and the other woman were supposed to go home for one final weekend and ask their spouses for a divorce. She did just that, but my husband did not. She got a quickie divorce fully expecting him to do the same. Upon returning to see her on Monday morning, he informed her that they were over and he was going to work towards reconciliation.

I accepted him back with no demands, save for the ones I told my God and one request of my husband. I did have him call her while I listened in to tell her again that it was over and he did. Most men that do come back do so with hard hearts, at first. I realize you DO deserve better! So did I. However, our response as wives makes all the difference. No demands meant that I accepted him as he was at the time.

My spouse told me that he had never loved me just to hurt me. He thought it would be easier to drive me away than work on our relationship. Then his words to me changed into more of an emphasis on the kids; "The kids don't deserve to live with us this way. They deserve better." When I did not give up on him, my spouse turned to focus on himself; "I hurt you. How can you forgive me?" God was softening his heart little by little until he finally gave in and admitted that he loved me (and always had).

My attitude made all the difference in God's ability to work in my spouse. I did not get in the way of His plan. Needless to say, I take NO credit for this. God shut my very vocal mouth and softened my heart. God deserves all the credit!

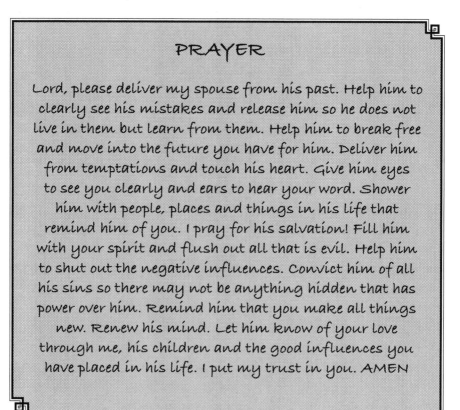

PRAYER

Lord, please deliver my spouse from his past. Help him to clearly see his mistakes and release him so he does not live in them but learn from them. Help him to break free and move into the future you have for him. Deliver him from temptations and touch his heart. Give him eyes to see you clearly and ears to hear your word. Shower him with people, places and things in his life that remind him of you. I pray for his salvation! Fill him with your spirit and flush out all that is evil. Help him to shut out the negative influences. Convict him of all his sins so there may not be anything hidden that has power over him. Remind him that you make all things new. Renew his mind. Let him know of your love through me, his children and the good influences you have placed in his life. I put my trust in you. AMEN

POWER

"A gentle answer turns away wrath, but a harsh word stirs up anger." (Proverbs 15:1)

"The path of the righteous is like the morning sun, shining ever brighter till the full light of day." (Proverbs 4:18)

Chapter 16

The Rose Garden and the Ring

When my spouse returned to reconcile there were no "I love you's". There were just "I'll live with you's." In fact, I was so tired from all of the stress and emotions that I decided to go with the kids to visit family in another state without him for two weeks, finally spending time with them. Incidentally, it is unfortunate that when your life is turned upside down, you spend all your energy and time dwelling on the situation, ignoring everyone else. This is a natural response but it was time for me to change my focus.

When I returned from the trip I discovered my spouse, on his days off from work, had built a beautiful rose garden in the backyard, just for me! He had made it from his own design, lugging heavy railroad ties to create two tiers. This thoughtful action was particularity special because ever since I was young I had always disliked Valentine's Day. People who didn't have a special someone watched others get gifts and those who did get flowers or something else most likely felt like the person HAD to buy them a gift. This was my opinion about the holiday, formed from my childhood. So . . . in the early part of our marriage I just asked for a rose bush every Valentine's Day, something I could plant and take care of and watch grow. I didn't get a single rose bush all those years. I figured he had just been too last minute with flowers/candy, didn't care, or didn't hear a single word I said. It was probably all three reasons!

<u>Finally</u> there was a light. I had many gorgeous rose bushes and a tired, sore, yet caring husband who had actually thought of me. He actually did something for <u>me</u> and not for the children or "others". This has become an outward sign of my husband's sincerity and hope. It is a continual sign of hope and of joy to care for the roses to this day. "Trust in the Lord with all your heart and lean not on your own understanding." (Proverbs 3:5)

———⁓⁓⚬⚬⚭⚬⚭⚬⚬⁓⁓———

I would love to say that my husband returned with open arms, pleading for my forgiveness and my everlasting love. That is definitely not how it went. I too had no big confessions of love or guilt, just a man standing before me saying that he was willing to try. He told me that he still did not love me, but that a friend had told him that love is a choice, and he was choosing me. OUCH! He still loved her and was struggling with not being with her, however, he felt like God wanted him with me. Now, I love God and want to do anything for Him . . . . But I wanted to be wanted for ME, not for God. So I went straight to the source.

I told my God exactly how I felt and I gave Him my list of requirements. The Lord clearly told me not to lay these stipulations on my husband, but to trust in His power to care for my needs. So, I obeyed. I had a long list of things I wanted to happen if I could ever believe in my spouse again. There were 10 things I needed. Over the years, nine of those requests were granted to me by the grace of God; all but one! The one was for "her" to apologize to me. Hahahaha . . . not happening, or God is still working on her!

The most important need I had was to renew our vows and get a new ring; one that would not be tainted with lies and deception, a symbol of a new start. On Christmas Eve that year, my husband staged an elaborate surprise. After the traditional midnight candlelight service at the church

I grew up in, we were married in, and all of my children were baptized in, he arranged for a vow renewal in the small chapel. I had no idea and was completely caught off guard. Unfortunately for me, he invited our immediate family to witness the event. It was kept simple and respectful, and my spouse presented me with a new ring. I have to admit, I was not at all ready for this step when it happened. At this point in our reconciliation, I was not even sure that I would say yes if ever asked again to be his wife. However, I was presented with a choice in a much unexpected way. I think I would have kept it private, however, this was my idea manifested by God himself, through my husband. WOW! Why do I ever doubt the Creator of the Universe? He is so amazing and knows me so well. God knew the timing would <u>have to be</u> His to get me to commit and accept my husband's recommitment. My faith had to be in God and not in any man on this earth.

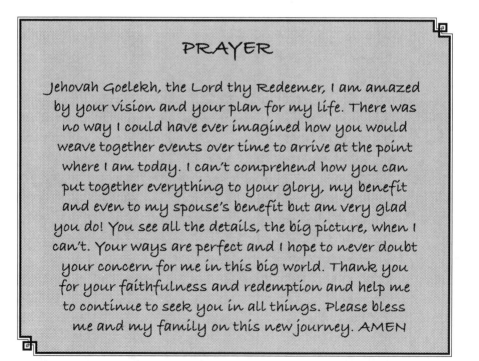

PRAYER

Jehovah Goelekh, the Lord thy Redeemer, I am amazed by your vision and your plan for my life. There was no way I could have ever imagined how you would weave together events over time to arrive at the point where I am today. I can't comprehend how you can put together everything to your glory, my benefit and even to my spouse's benefit but am very glad you do! You see all the details, the big picture, when I can't. Your ways are perfect and I hope to never doubt your concern for me in this big world. Thank you for your faithfulness and redemption and help me to continue to seek you in all things. Please bless me and my family on this new journey. AMEN

POWER

So he said to me, "This is the word of the Lord to Zerubbabel: 'Not by might nor by power, but by my Spirit,' says the Lord Almighty." (Zechariah 4:6)

"I have told you these things, so that in me you may have peace. In this world you will have trouble. But take heart! I have overcome the world." (John 16:33)

Chapter 17

That "Forgiveness" Word

"If my people, who are called by my name, will humble themselves and pray and seek my face and turn from their wicked ways, then I will hear from heaven, and I will forgive their sin and will heal their land." (2 Chronicles 7:14)

Attempt #1: Well . . . .
Attempt #2: Hmmm . . . .
Attempt #3: Ugh . . . .
I think I will let my dear friend address this chapter!

————————

Seeing as I cannot treat this chapter the same way as the Revenge chapter, I guess I will have to try another approach.

Let's just be honest. This is a yucky and unfair topic to talk about. It is wrong, yet it is just right. It is hard, yet the concept is simple. It can release you, but can you release it? Read that again . . . It can release <u>you</u>, but can you release <u>it</u>? The healing powers of forgiveness are immense and eternal, but getting there is the struggle. You do not want to, nor should you have to by the standards of this world. However, by my faith's standards and what is right for me, I must forgive. Ugh! It seems impossible, and very well may be, without help.

The only way to begin the forgiveness process, and rest assured that it is a process, is to get your big toe wet. Just start. Just wade into the water a tiny bit, and then run back if it is too cold. You may even get in up to your knees or waist and have to head for the shore. It is alright! The ocean is not moving and neither is the vast ocean of forgiveness.

Begin by praying that God help you. Ask Him to help you forgive as an act of God's will, not your own. Ask Him to make your will like His. Slowly but surely He will guide you down the shore and into the water inch by inch.

Remember that forgiving is not a release of guilt or responsibility from you to your spouse. It is simply your personal acknowledgement of the wrong that has been done to you and a decision to move forward with healing. The Merriam-Webster dictionary defines forgiveness as a verb:

FORGIVENESS:

1. *a: to give up resentment of or claim to requital for <forgive an insult>*
   b: to grant relief from payment of <forgive a debt>
2. *to cease to feel resentment against (an offender): pardon <forgive one's enemies>*

I personally like 1.b . . . It means to not only grant yourself relief, but also your spouse from intense resentment. You will never think it is alright, or understand, or excuse the act of betrayal. However, the sense of "granting relief" can place some of the power back into your hands and give one portion of control back to you. You do have the ability and the power, with <u>God's help</u>, to forgive. You do not have to rush in. It is a process that will take many years of work. You will likely have to forgive him every day anew until it "takes". Give it time!

PRAYER

El-nose, a forgiving God, help me to find forgiveness
in this unforgiving world. Forgive me for my
unclean thoughts, anger, and doubt. I release my
emotions to you . . . by your will and not my own.
You forgive us for our sins instantly because we are
your children and you are a just God. You are perfect
but we are not. I know that not forgiving someone
hurts me more. I long for the relief that comes with
true forgiveness. Teach me your way. AMEN

POWER

"A Levite and His Concubine: One of the biblical
examples of forgiveness in Adultery:

In those days Israel had no king. Now a Levite who
lived in a remote area in the hill country of Ephraim
took a concubine from Bethlehem in Judah. But she was
unfaithful to him. She left him and went back to her
parents' home in Bethlehem, Judah. After she had been
there four months, her husband went to her to persuade
her to return. He had with him his servant and two
donkeys. She took him into her parents' home, and
when her father saw him, he gladly welcomed him. His
father-in-law, the woman's father, prevailed on him to
stay; so he remained with him three days, eating and
drinking, and sleeping there." (Judges 19:1-4)

Chapter 18

Repercussions/Trust

"Let us not become weary in doing good,
for at the proper time we will reap a harvest
if we do not give up." (Galatians 6:9)

Satan AND God have a plan for your life. I do not feel that it is enough to simply learn about God. I feel you also have to know your enemy. You are not fighting your spouse and you are not fighting yourself, you are in a spiritual battle with Satan. God is big and powerful enough to win the war, battle by battle, with your constant prayers. I learned a lot about intercessory prayer and the power of it. If you ask God for big things and have big faith you will receive big things. If you ask him for little things because you have little faith then you shall receive little.

Now to discuss the repercussions . . . God is a just God and if your spouse returns he will have to live with the fallout and face friends, family and acquaintances. After all he did tell everyone that he didn't love you and wasn't happy and so on. This will be hard on them and they will have to become humble. Somehow, you will have to refrain from throwing things back in their face all of the time! I suggest researching all there is to know about 'taming the tongue' in the Bible.

Although it will be tough on him, it will be harder on you! My spouse was relieved because he wasn't running away or rebelling anymore and said he didn't need to continue counseling because he knew what he wanted and was fine. On the other hand, I was NOT fine and continued going to counseling for a while. I was repulsed by him at this point, had no love for anyone and wondered how I was going to make it through the day. Life became easier as the months went by, thank goodness.

LIES, LIES, LIES, oh those stinking LIES! Your spouse will have told you lie after lie and then told you more lies to cover up the previous lies until they are even lying about what they ate for lunch because they weren't supposed to be there! They get really good at it and actually convince themselves that this "lie" could be true or I need to tell my spouse this "lie" so that I don't hurt them more. Unfortunately, by the time they return home you have become really good at snooping and rummaging through cell phones, suitcases, emails, and cars (to name a few), basically becoming obsessive. Years down the road you will not have looked anywhere and then all of a sudden it will hit you and you just 'look'. You hope to not find anything, but from experience, oddities could be there. You see, when they return you beg and plead for them to tell you everything, all the deceit, so that you don't have to re-live the pain over and over again when you find out something new. They still don't tell you everything. Thus, you will discover that they will "have to" continue to lie on a much smaller scale "to protect your feelings." I have to say that sometimes the lies are worse than the act itself because how can you trust your spouse again!?

Well, there is good news. If you prayed continuously and it was a God-thing that your spouse returned, then you don't have to trust your spouse. You just need to put your trust in God and God alone. Trust God to show you if they stray again. Trust God to help you get through the next minute. Trust God that your best interest is in His hands. Trust God to help you build a strong marriage over time. Trust God.

It is impossible to encounter destruction of any kind without fallout . . .

- ✓ "What goes up must come down."—*Newton, Isaac*
- ✓ "To every action there is always opposed an equal reaction."—*Newton, Isaac*
- ✓ "What goes around comes around."—I refuse to give Karma credit here, although that is where the world thinks this quote comes from. It originates from Isaiah 3:11, Matthew 7:12, Proverbs 26:27, Galatians 6:7, etc.

I could go on with the clichés and quotes, but you get my drift. As I have stated in previous chapters, any decision is a hard one and any choice is not one you want to make, or ever dreamed of making. I always say that I am in a lose/lose situation. Fortunately, that is not all true, but it sure feels like it most of the time. What I do with my future is up to me. Who I choose to be is within my power. Yes, my choices stink, but I will one day get over that and be glad for the choice I make if I am sure that my decision is founded in Christ. That being said, I am going to address the other end of repercussions or consequences. YOU! You will experience the fallout even more drastically than the unfaithful spouse will. These unfortunate events will continue for quite some time and they will be a thorn in your side.

The immediate consequences of his actions for me were the obvious depression, embarrassment, pain, loss, job insecurity, instability, reactions from the kids and family, etc . . . The lasting ones are what I want to focus on. A "friend" once told me "*You* decided to stay with the guy. Now get over it!" That friend almost lost valuable body parts that day. He was thinking from a standpoint that I needed to move on with the healing and restoration, but he did not word it correctly at all! This idea is impossible to discuss unless you have been there! Yes, I agree that I need to move forward, but there are those moments when I cannot. I call these times *triggers*. They are tiny things that are said or done (by anyone at all) that remind me of the pain and transport me right back to those horrific days. A quick list off the top of my head would be . . .

- ✓ Movies
- ✓ Music lyrics
- ✓ Sermon topics
- ✓ Locations
- ✓ Smells
- ✓ Sounds
- ✓ Getting the phone bill
- ✓ Attitudes
- ✓ Phone ringing

. . . *a few of my "triggers".*

So basically everything and anything in a day can trigger a bad thought or memory. It is exhausting! DO NOT think this is wrong. It just is . . . and there is nothing you can do to prevent it. The only thing you can do is react in a controlled way. The best I can do when these triggers take my breath away, is to give myself a personal time out. My spouse knows that when he asks what is wrong and I tell him I am just having a thought or a moment, he is to back off. If he does not give me space, I will blow up at him and throw it in his face. That is only natural, and let's face it; you deserve to be allowed to. Truth is that it only hurts you in the end by taking your recovery back a step. After some time, my husband always comes back over to me and asks if there is anything he can do to help. That is one thing he does right.

Triggers often get resolved or fade away with time. I am better able to listen to music now and most of the time I do not freak out at the inevitable affair scene on TV or in a movie. Getting better, I do believe! This is a spiritual battle for your marriage, children and your very soul. Be in control as much as you can and let God have control of it all!

PRAYER

Elohim Lacham, God who fights for me, I acknowledge that these struggles I face are a battle for my soul. I belong to you! There are many obstacles that my spouse and I face daily. I know these obstacles can break us down or be used for your glory. Help us to draw on your strength and focus on the bigger picture for our future instead of dwelling on the past. Lord, I need you to take control of my thoughts and to tame my tongue so that I am able to heal. Please turn all the lies into truths so that trust can be re-established. Help this fight to not be with myself but standing with you against Satan and his attempts to tear me down! AMEN

POWER

"The one who is in you is greater than the one who is in the world." (1 John 4:4)

"But blessed is the one who trusts in the Lord, whose confidence is in him." (Jeremiah 17:7)

Chapter 19

'The Holy Spirit Poops' and Other Miracles

"At that time Jesus came from Nazareth in Galilee and was baptized by John in the Jordan. As Jesus was coming up out of the water, he saw heaven being torn open and the Spirit descending on him like a dove." (Mark 1:9-10)

There will come a day when you have had enough, when you have prayed and cried and prayed some more and you are just "DONE". The second round (noted in *Updates*, Chapter 20) I prayed and listened and hoped for an entire year and then I hit bottom. I felt like it was all up to God now and I needed a life boat. I begged and cried to God for hours to just rescue me. To just send me some sign . . . desperately needing to be rescued from my situation. I was tired of finding out about things and tired of trying to make sense out of anything and "going through" the process. I was tired of trying to follow scripture and seeing hope in the situation and then nothing. I needed to feel peace and not be attached in any way to the hope my spouse would change. God heard me. God knew I was soooooo incredibly tired and needed to be freed. I told God He was definitely in control and it was ALL His now. He heard me, He sent me a sign, and He is an AWESOME GOD. This is my story, this is my song . . .

It was a Thursday when I cried out to the Lord for hours for a life boat, a miracle, a sign. I wanted a sign of something, not really sure of what, just a sign. Friday early afternoon came along and my daughter called me to the living room to see a pigeon that showed up out of the blue and was hanging out by our back porch, knocking on the window slightly with his beak. We watched for a while and hoped it would go away because pigeons poop! We didn't know how it got there or where it came from because we just had black birds, squirrels and lizards who hung out around our home. Hours went by and it still was there. It wasn't afraid of us or the Golden Retriever we let out. Nothing was wrong with it. The pigeon could fly so nothing was wrong with its wings. We had a fenced in yard and lived in a subdivision. It was like it was guarding our home. The pigeon slept through the night right near the corner of our two sliding glass doors. It was so unusual that I kept thinking about it all night and wondered if it meant anything. I knew pigeons were commonly known as messengers.

So Saturday, the next morning, I looked on Wikipedia under 'pigeons.' I was immediately drawn to the paragraph saying the words 'pigeon' and 'dove' were interchangeable. I had a Rock Dove on my back deck! Not only that but one section in Wikipedia mentioned that "In the book of Genesis, Noah sent out a dove after the great flood to determine how far the floodwaters had receded. *"Dove"* is also a term of endearment in the Song of Songs and elsewhere. In Hebrew, Jonah means dove. The *"sign of Jonas" in Matthew 16:1-4* is related to the *"sign of the dove"* And *"the Holy Spirit descended upon Jesus at his baptism like a dove"* (Matthew 3:16), and subsequently the *"peace dove"* became a common Christian symbol of the Holy Spirit." What?! I had the Holy Spirit guarding my door and it poops!

Obviously, at this point I went straight to Matthew 16:1-4 in the Bible seeking more answers and of course the title of the chapter is "Leaders Demand a Miraculous Sign." Verses 1-4 state, *"The Pharisees and Sadducees came to Jesus and tested him by asking him to show them a sign from heaven. He replied,*

"When evening comes, you say, 'It will be fair weather, for the sky is red,' and in the morning, 'Today it will be stormy, for the sky is red and overcast.' You know how to interpret the appearance of the sky, but you cannot interpret the signs of the times. A wicked and adulteress generation looks for a miraculous sign, but none will be given it except the sign of Jonah." Jesus then left them and went away." The dove showed up on my deck early Friday afternoon right before the storm that The Weather Channel didn't mention was coming over our area. In fact two storms came through unexpectedly.

By now I didn't know whether I was going crazy or God was sending me the sign I begged for. Just to be sure I ran it by my daughter and talked to a friend. Both said it was a sign. I looked out the window again and there was a "red bird". One of my friends told me a story that during her struggles, she saw a "red bird" cross her path and to her it was a sign of Hope. So now I had Peace (the dove) and Hope (the red bird) but still wondered if it was all a coincidence.

About 30 minutes later, I looked outside and a long black SNAKE appeared on my deck near my lawn chair! It was as if God said in heaven "Man this girl is thick headed . . . cue the snake!" because I was still wondering if I had a message from God. So there I sat looking out the sliding glass door at the long, black snake AND the dove who was still guarding my door. Did the snake represent Satan? I watched the dove waddle to one end of my outdoor table furniture to look at the snake and then back to the corner and then to the other side of the furniture and back to the corner. He never flew away.

I started to panic because I didn't want the snake to kill my dove! My other thought was that if the dove represented the Holy Spirit, and the snake represented Satan, the dove would ultimately win in battle because Good conquers Evil, right? But how would that happen??? Neither animal was leaving! I decided to throw my dog's toys at the snake to get it to leave. It didn't leave. It just lifted its head and looked at me. I then took the hose out and turned it on jet and sprayed it. The snake just lifted its head again and moved slightly. YIKES!!! What now??!!

I called Christine and told her to come over because this was just getting unbelievable and I needed her to see it for herself. She came over and was in awe. She actually ran down the street but I told her she didn't need to do that because the Holy Spirit and Satan weren't going anywhere! I showed her the information I found in the Bible and Wikipedia and our spirits were lifted! It gets better . . .

We asked her husband to come down and get rid of the snake because neither one of us was going to touch it, so he came straight down. He walked outside over to the snake and nudged it. It didn't move. He then exclaimed that it was dead. What??? DEAD???!!! How could it be dead??? Satan is DEAD!!! God won! The battle is over! Phew! The snake had apparently just died in the last 10 minutes without any visible sign of trauma or injury to it at all! What???!!! I'm sorry but a long black snake just doesn't appear every day, or any day, on my deck and dies just like that while a dove is guarding my door. The snake just died! I seriously could hear God in heaven saying, "Do you get it now?" I literally felt like I had just watched a live Christian play starring animal actors. Christine said that I had better believe that it was a message from God now or else the next thing He would send would be locusts and she certainly didn't want that to happen!

The commentary in my Bible concerning Matthew 16:4 states, "Many people, like these Jewish leaders, say they want to see a miracle so that they can believe. But Jesus knew that miracles never convince the skeptical. Jesus had been healing, raising people from the dead, and feeding thousands, and still people wanted him to prove himself. Do you doubt Christ because you haven't seen a miracle? Do you expect God to prove himself to you personally before you believe? Jesus says, '*Blessed are those who have not seen and yet have believed*' (John 20:29). We have all the miracles recorded in the Old and New Testaments, 2,000 years of church history, and the witness of thousands. With all this evidence, those who won't believe are either too proud or too stubborn. If you simply step forward in faith and believe, then you will begin to see the miracles that God can do with your life!"

My spouse walked into the house Saturday morning briefly and saw just a pigeon that would stay as long as we gave it food and water. I saw a miracle. I saw a sign. I heard a message from God. I saw and felt the power of the Holy Spirit. I finally felt the peace I had been longing for. I knew God was real. I knew He was listening. I knew He was protecting my home. I knew change was coming and I knew that whatever changes occurred, it would be part of the plan God had set out for me.

Today is Monday. I let the dog out at 6am and looked in the darkness to see if my blessed dove was still there. It was . . . in the corner by the two glass doors. I looked again at 7:30am. My dove was gone. He had stayed with us for the entire weekend but at the light of day on Monday he left. I don't know where he came from and I don't know where he went and that really doesn't matter but I can assure you that, "AS FOR ME AND MY HOUSE, WE WILL SERVE THE LORD." (Joshua 24:15)

Guardian Angel

Slithering Snake

Redbird of Hope

The Battle
The Dove and the Snake

Little Big Miracles for Christine . . .

"He performs wonders that cannot be fathomed, miracles that cannot be counted. He provides rain for the earth; he sends water on the countryside. The lowly he sets on high and those who mourn are lifted to safety." (Job 5:9-11)

1. The Lord has always been so faithful to give me what I need, when I needed it. When I KNEW that my husband had something to tell me and was not talking . . . I searched and found nothing. Until, I finally asked the One who knows, to show me *IF* I needed to know. I put the control in His hands. Online, I stumbled upon a picture of a woman and I knew it was her *and* that he was having an affair. I do not know how, only that God showed me! It was true, and when my husband asked me how I knew, all I could tell him was that God showed me, because that is all of the hard evidence I had. Amazing!

2. You know that pit in your stomach feeling that just won't go away? You know something is wrong but you have no hard proof, so you drop to your knees? When I knew that I knew my husband should not get in the car to go on that weekend trip, I put it in God's hands. I prayed that God would stop him if my feelings were correct, or quiet my heart if it was just my worrying. Well, the God of the heavens and all creation obviously knows a little something about cars, too. His car threw a rod, rendering it inoperable!!! Not only that, but he was nearest to me and even called me to come and get him. At this point he was not calling me unless he wanted to see the kids. God was able to stop him, where I was not. God was able to draw my husband's heart to ME!

101

3. Shortly after my husband moved out, God spoke again. I was at a church banquet, minding my own business. The pastor gave a sermon on tithing, as we were ready to expand our ever growing church family. I sat wrestling with God for the entire sermon. I asked Him, "How can you mean this for someone like me, with no income, two kids and an estranged husband? I have no money left over after paying all the bills and the expense of his new living arrangements." The burden was just too much to bear. There was no money. All I had was my spouse's money and he was at least being kind enough to continue paying the bills, I could not ask for more! God had a plan! God told me that if I were to give $200 a month, he would provide it. Of course, I continued to argue with Him, but came to the conclusion that if God wanted me to do this, I had enough faith in Him to obey. So I told the Lord that if He would show me $200 each month, I would give it gladly. After, the service was over and I was packing my Bible away to go and get my children from the nursery, the miracle occurred. A man that I had never formally met approached me. He told me that while he was ironing his shirt for church that evening, God spoke to him. He told him to give the new member, Christine, a check for $200. He continued to apologize saying he had no idea why I needed the money, nor did he mean any insult to me. He was just doing as told. Did you read that correctly? $200! The exact amount God placed in my head that night! I gave that money the next morning in church with a peaceful and joyful heart. Since that day, we have tithed and have always found the 10%!

PRAYER

Gelah Raz, a revealer of mysteries, WOW!!! Thank you for your miracles, small and big. Help us to remember that if our faith is big then we will ask for big things and watch you move mountains. Your glory continues to amaze me! No matter how long I have on this earth, I know that I will want to spend it with you. In you are my hope, my peace, and my comfort. AMEN

POWER

"You are the God who performs miracles; you display your power among the peoples." (Psalm 77:14)

Chapter 20

Updates

"Consider it pure joy, my brothers and sisters, whenever you face trials of many kinds because you know that the testing of your faith produces perseverance. Let perseverance finish its work so that you may be mature and complete, not lacking anything." (James 1:2-4)

Lynn

The first year of reconciliation was tough because doubt and mistrust surfaced frequently for me. My husband, though, seemed fine, as I said before, even though he had to face friends and family when he made the decision to be faithful and be a family again. He also had to answer all of my relentless questions bred from insecurities.

A couple of years went by and I didn't go back into the work force so that I could remain a constant source of stability for everyone. He would be able to come home on his days off and spend time with us rather than worrying about responsibilities here. One day, however, when his work stopped hiring and was reducing operations, shifting people around, he was told he needed to commute to work. It would probably be for only about three months. Three months turned into five years. Five years of only being home two days during the week. Five years of working weekends and not being able to go church with us. Five years spending time at work with other people who didn't go to church either. Five years of essentially living out of a suitcase! And of course I felt even stronger about not going back to work but continued to stay at home, providing the stability he and my kids needed. I did, however, do volunteer work, stay involved with the kids' schools, and manage a few properties.

Then came the dreadful day. The day I asked for his insurance card so that I could fill out our car registration form. He nonchalantly handed me his wallet and a note caught my eye. It was a note written to someone else and was obviously a very 'friendly' note. Awesome . . . unfaithfulness again. He tried, for just a minute, to explain it away but quickly figured out that he was getting nowhere and said he was going to ask for a divorce after the summer. It was April. Needless to say he was out of the house again that day, staying in hotels whenever he was back in town. Then in August, he finally rented an apartment.

This time when I prayed there was no question that I would be following God's leading. The only thing I heard from God was just to pray for his salvation. That was it. So that is what I have been doing for the last year and will continue to do no matter what and no matter how long! The old horrible emotions and stages came flooding back. I have been on a rollercoaster ride for a long time but still give control over to God when it comes to my future. I began talking to Christine shortly after finding out. Then, when her husband "fell" again we were led through prayer to gather our writings from before and forge ahead in writing this book so that others would know they are not alone. We all have different experiences, financial situations, and family issues, but staying close to God and listening to His teachings through the Holy Spirit are what bind us together. We have noticed that the closer we get to completing this book, the harder Satan attacks, so we have been praying fervently for protection.

My journey is far from over . . . in fact, a new chapter is just beginning. I am still separated but have started school again to update my skills and have since replanted my rose garden on my own. It remains my source of joy and hope in the Lord because of the love and care that first built it. I pray every day, many times, for my husband and always will. You, my friends, by reading this book, have also become a part of my future!

—⁓⁓⁓⁓⁓⁓⁓⁓⁓—

Christine

Fifteen years later and two more children, I was really doing well. I actually said to myself in my reflection time that I was really and finally over most of the issues that had arisen as a result of the affair with "her". I had a marriage that others envied. We were continuing to date, flirt and had a very healthy relationship. Our kids were doing quite well; they were all teenagers and our house was still standing. We were the house that all the kids wanted to hang out at, and yet we always found family time and time for just the two of us. Personally, I was finally able to be me again. The kids were able to care for themselves in the evening if I had to go somewhere. My life was coming together nicely in these later years of mommy-hood.

My husband's travel had been a lot less lately and we were really enjoying having him around more. So when we found out that he had a two week trip coming up, it was hard. We spent time together to prepare, and off he went. Upon his return, I picked him up at the airport only to find him still in "business mode". Avoiding any real time together, He took me to see some of his work in the area. Strangely, he became extremely agitated when a normal argument broke out with our oldest daughter via phone. I chalked it all up to being away for two weeks. When we arrived home, out of nowhere, he decided he wanted to join my entire extended family at the lake house for the weekend. He wanted to leave that night. Now, for years he had not wanted to go to the lake, and especially after being on a business trip. I also found it strange because I knew we would be sleeping on one of 3 futons in the family room with my two sisters and their spouses; not exactly the welcome home I was prepared to provide. Major red flag; at this point I was concerned! The entire weekend he was distant. He hardly spoke to me and stayed on the boat away from me as much as he could. It hurt so badly and on the way home I confronted him about it.

For the next two months he was hardly there. The man I thought I knew so well was beating himself up inside for the choice he had made and he was so afraid that I was going to find out. His guilt and fear tormented him. He would work long hours and have every excuse in the world to stay away. He always blamed me for being unsympathetic to his job; that was so far from the truth. When he did come home, he would say he had more work to do in the home office, and he would disappear for the night at his desk. Every night he would pour himself multiple drinks, which he had never done before. He was drinking like a fish and I was trying to keep up so as to do something with him. I could not hold as much as he could, needless to say. This was scary.

Finally it happened. My husband drank his nights ration and said he was tired and wanted to go to bed early. When he got in the bed I went to tuck him in as usual. When I walked in to the room, I sat down beside him to tell him I loved him and kiss him good night. Going in for the kiss, I felt his pillow vibrate . . . his pillow. Reaching under his pillow, I found his phone. He quickly grabbed it from me in sheer panic. I said for him to let me see it and he looked into my eyes with a cold, hard look and sternly told me "NO". My heart dropped and I knew. I left the room expecting him to follow . . . but I sat on the couch alone for what seemed quite a while (a clue, a clue). I think it was only 20 minutes in reality. I was in a perpetual gasp wondering how this could be. Was I really here . . . again? No . . . I was over reacting . . . but I knew I was not. I could barely breathe. My whole life was crashing in on me and I felt so betrayed and bewildered. Everything in me wanted to deny what I knew but something wouldn't let me.

He finally came out of the bedroom with a defensive attitude (clue # gazillion) saying that he did not know what he had to do to please me; that I knew what was happening with work and that I was not being understanding and why in the world could I not just trust him. Hadn't he been great the last 15 years? Didn't that count for anything? What was my problem? He went to bed and I sat staring at the wall for hours. The next few days were business as usual, except we were even more distant and I was always wondering.

I began searching everything I could to find answers. Obsession filled my days and it was driving me mad; always looking and thinking about what might be going on and what would happen to me and the kids. Finally I was desperate and exhausted and I truly cried out to God. I asked Him to allow me to rest in the truth. I wanted God to show me what the truth was if He would have me know. If He did not want me to know, I would just stop torturing myself and move on. I completely gave it to the Lord.

I suppose He wanted me to know. As I was building my own social web business account, I found and "friended" my husband. I scrolled through his friend list and I saw her face; and I knew instantly. I had no hard evidence, no messages that I could find to incriminate him. I just knew. I text my husband that I knew and he needed to tell me if he loved her or not. He tried to deny it and then he fell silent; he knew he was caught. He admitted it was her and told me it was a one night stand and he did not love her. It was over for them both, apparently. But it had only begun for me. After I screamed to God and cried to Lynn, he arrived home. I instantly jumped up and exploded on him. That night we told the teens what their daddy had done and that we did not know what was to happen in the future. The kids and I agreed that he should not stay in our home that night, so he left for a hotel. And so began my next journey of agony and betrayal, anger and hatred, fear and uncertainty, unreal strength and sinking weakness. Where do I go now?

However, if you think there is more to this story, you are right. There is a feeling that a woman gets down deep in the pit of her very being that tells her that it is not over. There is almost always more to the story than he is able to admit. Through searching, I found all of the emails following the affair. They were flirtatious and sickening. This is where I could have sworn I was done, really done. The reasoning for his continuation of the affair was debatable and sketchy at best, but the point for me was the lies that had encased our last few months. Those months were filled with my efforts to put myself back together while he was trying to keep her together, while "she" was falling apart. He described her now as scary and psychotic, and yet he felt the need to comfort her. I felt like this was to save himself, but I didn't really know.

My point here is that you never have all of the answers. That is so hard to grasp. The pain and betrayal has no reason or rhyme. The more I try to reason it away, the more I am frustrated. I have come to the conclusion that I cannot and will not understand all that is out there. Some things I need to just give to God and trust in His understanding. That is the best I can do.

What truly matters is what I decide to do for me in the days that I have left. Is God going to be in control, or am I? I say that because we have no idea how much time we have on this earth; we need to embrace all that we can and live life abundantly. Difficult as that is, I will (mind over matter) strive to make my life and future what the Lord and I always dreamed it to be. I hope he gets his act straight and is alongside of me. If not, I will still be me and I will be O.K.

PRAYER

Yasha, my Savior, from this day forward, we vow to stand together and keep looking toward the heavens for direction in all that we do. It is our desire to encourage others in strength and righteousness through our struggles and when we fall into doubt and despair, help us to support one another and redirect our paths. Take all our "gifts" and failures and use them to your glory. Help others to relate to and learn from our choices, good and bad. Lord, you know I am not perfect. Thank you for your sacrifice and unfailing love! "Praise be to the Lord, to God our Savior, who daily bears our burdens." (Psalm 68:19) AMEN

POWER

"Some of you will rebuild the deserted ruins of your cities. Then you will be known as a rebuilder of walls and a restorer of homes." (Isaiah 58:12)

"Stop deceiving yourselves. If you think you are wise by this world's standards, you need to become a fool to be truly wise." (1 Corinthians 3:18)

"For God was in Christ, reconciling the world to himself, no longer counting people's sins against them. And he gave us this wonderful message of reconciliation." (2 Corinthians 5:19)

"Wait for the Lord; be strong and take heart and wait for the Lord." (Psalm 27:14)

"Don't have anything to do with foolish and stupid arguments, because you know they produce quarrels." (2 Timothy 2:23)

Chapter 21

Your Story: YOUR Witness

"I long to see you that I may impart to you some spiritual gift to make you strong—that is, that you and I may be mutually encouraged by each other's faith."(Romans 1:11-12)

It is amazing how many people will open up to you if they discover you really do not have the perfect life . . . the white picket fence syndrome. Sometimes I wonder if we actually did have the perfect family life and he had the dream job and everything was good, so he just needed to create his own problems for a change of pace and excitement. However, those rebellious acts almost cost him everything that is really important . . . and still could.

During this time God had planned for me to be so close to His word that through my struggles I could help anyone. He has put several people in my path to encourage. So many marriages are affected by infidelity! The stories can be similar or very different but how YOU respond, allowing God to work or allowing what the world says to do take precedence, makes all the difference. I wrote a lot down in a journal and started writing a couple of pages in the hopes of sharing with people someday about all that I discovered on my walk with God but when Thanksgiving rolled around that year and he was back in the house trying to move forward from the past, I stopped writing because it hurt too much to re-live all the memories.

It wasn't until the second time around for me and a short time later for Christine that we decided to join forces and write this book. Admittedly it has been quite a struggle to sit and write and that is because the subject matter is too close to home! We continue having to keep each other accountable not only to continue writing, but for staying true to God's word while going through our current struggles. (It would be nice to just be "rescued" from them once though ☺).

She had writings from before as well, and so with God's blessing and nudging, we spent months putting into words our experiences in the hopes that someday we could 'be there' for a Christian spouse during a time of confusion, insecurity, and stress. Some people we know who have gone through infidelity in their marriage have counseled others in their churches and have shared in front of groups or to individuals . . . where is your ministry?

———————

Never in a million years, with all of the gifts I am blessed with did I ever think I would be where I am today. My fairy tale was not supposed to end this way. My life was set up to be the American dream and now my dream feels like more of a nightmare.

I have faith that it will be restored to me and I will live my alternate reality of happily ever after. This drive in me, with God, to return to my happy place is exactly why I wanted to join forces with Lynn to write this book.

I, too, had written papers and help booklets from my first experience that were intended to be passed out to those I encountered in this situation. I was fortunate enough to be used of God in several marriages. For that, I Praise the Lord. I am willing to be used. If Lynn and I were to go through all of this and never bring glory to the name of the Lord, it would be impossible to have hope. Only He knows my future and what new joys it holds. Our obedience largely determines our outcome.

For me, I continue to learn and heal each day. There are still trigger days, but they seem to be farther apart each time. I am working toward enjoying my everyday life again! 'Praise The Lord' Family time seems a little more playful and we even had an anniversary trip that went well. Good things!

I truly hope that you, the reader, are healed and whole very soon. In the meantime, we have composed this book to help you feel normal, understood and able to carry on. I find immense comfort in knowing anything I tell Lynn will not be outlandish or unfamiliar to her. She feels my pain in a way that many cannot. We hope to be that for you. You are NOT alone and you CAN do it, with God's help!

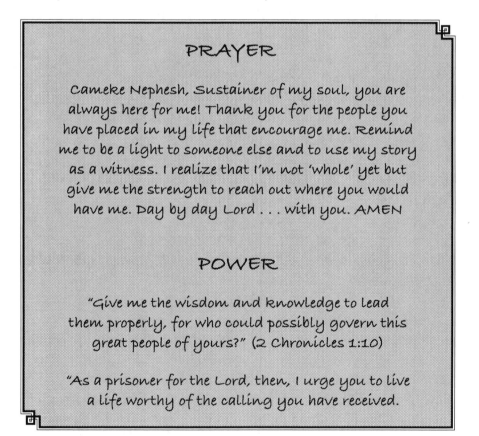

PRAYER

Cameke Nephesh, Sustainer of my soul, you are always here for me! Thank you for the people you have placed in my life that encourage me. Remind me to be a light to someone else and to use my story as a witness. I realize that I'm not 'whole' yet but give me the strength to reach out where you would have me. Day by day Lord . . . with you. AMEN

POWER

"Give me the wisdom and knowledge to lead them properly, for who could possibly govern this great people of yours?" (2 Chronicles 1:10)

"As a prisoner for the Lord, then, I urge you to live a life worthy of the calling you have received.

Be completely humble and gentle; be patient, bearing with one another in love. Make every effort to keep the unity of the Spirit through the bond of peace. There is one body and one Spirit—just as you were called to one hope when you were called—one Lord, one faith, one baptism; one God and Father of all, who is over all and through all and in all." (Ephesians 1-6) (People are watching you. Can they see Christ in you?)

"I will make you into a great nation and I will bless you; I will make your name great, and you will be a blessing. I will bless those who bless you, and whoever curses you I will curse; and all the peoples on earth will be blessed through you." (Genesis 12:2-3)

"In everything I did, I showed you that by this kind of hard work we must help the weak, remembering the words the Lord Jesus himself said: 'It is more blessed to give than to receive.'" (Acts 20:35)

"I pray that your partnership with us in the faith may be effective in deepening your understanding of every good thing we share for the sake of Christ." (Philemon 1:6)

Chapter 22

A Parting Word from Us Girls . . .

*"I'm eager to encourage you in your faith, but I also
want to be encouraged by yours. In this way, each
of us will be a blessing to the other." (Romans 1:12)*

To my precious friends,

Never, ever, ever, ever forget you are a child of God. You are important and special. You are worth more to the Lord and to others than you can imagine or will ever know. Whether you stay married or face divorce, the Lord is there with you and has a plan for your life, and if you stay close to Him you can't go wrong. Sometimes you may feel that you can't make it through another minute! You don't have to. That is the time to just make it through the next 30 seconds and then when you have accomplished that, get through the next 30 minutes and when you do that, then get through the next hour and so on. You don't need to stress about what tomorrow may bring when "each day has enough trouble of its own." (Matthew 6:34)

When trying to get through something remember that you are not in control, sing praises for the blessings you have, and trust that God has a plan. In the still moments listen to the Holy Spirit's leading for your next step and always be open to God using you as an instrument. Pray for the right words and for peace in the midst of the storm. You will be okay if you stay with God. It is human nature to disappoint so putting trust in a person, does not always works. God never disappoints. Trust in Him and Him alone.

If you know you have done everything possible as a Christian, cut yourself a break. Your spouse makes his own choices and God can save him without your help. Imagining that your spouse will ride off into the sunset with another and be truly happy is a farce. That person will have to live with himself knowing what he has done and the pain his actions caused. It might be time to focus only on God not your spouse. If you have kids, love them dearly every day and teach them what you have learned in your walk. You will be blessed for your faithfulness. That is a promise. Love to you all!

In Christ,
Lynne

―――――∿∽∘◯⦾◯◯⦿◯◯∘∽∿―――――

"After Job had prayed for his friends, the Lord restored his fortunes and gave him twice as much as he had before." (Job 42:10)

Ladies, ladies, ladies,

This stinks and there is no water for the bath!! But you are lucky . . . because Lynn and I have some body spray to cover the stink of the moment and get you through to tomorrow. One day, God will pour down sweet rain, like a cleansing flood and render you clean, healed and restored, in His name. Until then, He has provided daily encouragement for you in the form of friends, this book, praise music, and the Word!

If the Lord had not seen ahead to provide me with Lynn in the midst of all of this, I dare say I would not be married, sane or possibly even alive right now. This book never would have been possible without our joined efforts to survive! That is exactly what this time in your life is—survival!

I cannot express how much you need to only focus on one day at a time, really, one minute at a time. Tomorrow will take care of itself. You must survive this and come out on top, with

God's awesome help. Allow Him to guide you as only He can. Ask God not only for daily bread, but for all your needs and even a dessert some times. He longs to give us what we need and what we want; to see us happy and fulfilled. We only have to ask, trust and wait on Him. (I hate the word wait!) You can do it!

In Jesus name,
Christine

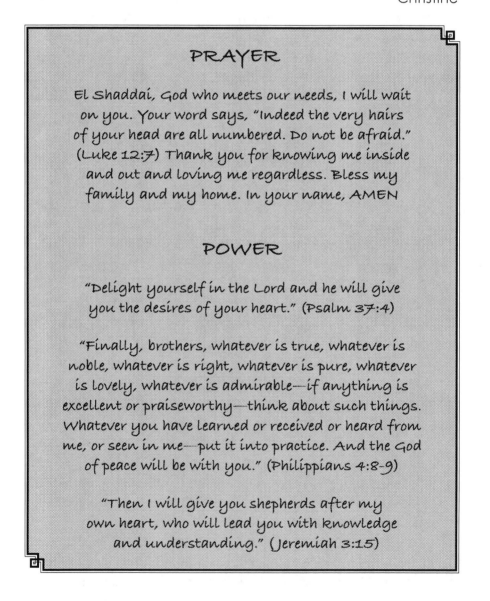

PRAYER

El Shaddai, God who meets our needs, I will wait on you. Your word says, "Indeed the very hairs of your head are all numbered. Do not be afraid." (Luke 12:7) Thank you for knowing me inside and out and loving me regardless. Bless my family and my home. In your name, AMEN

POWER

"Delight yourself in the Lord and he will give you the desires of your heart." (Psalm 37:4)

"Finally, brothers, whatever is true, whatever is noble, whatever is right, whatever is pure, whatever is lovely, whatever is admirable—if anything is excellent or praiseworthy—think about such things. Whatever you have learned or received or heard from me, or seen in me—put it into practice. And the God of peace will be with you." (Philippians 4:8-9)

"Then I will give you shepherds after my own heart, who will lead you with knowledge and understanding." (Jeremiah 3:15)

Chapter 23

From the Mouths of Babes

"For the creation waits in eager expectation for the children of God to be revealed."(Romans 8:19)

Through the eyes of a child:

The goal of the children writing is to help the parent reader, or the child, understand the perspective of children of multiple age groups, different families, and genders. It is by no means to voice negative remarks . . . just real honest thoughts and emotions. These thoughts and emotions are their individual perspectives about what happened in their families. The replies to the questions are neither right nor wrong. They are very normal and to be expected. These precious children are not alone!

1. What was your initial reaction and the first thought that went through your mind? How are you now?
2. Who or what helped you through this time?
3. What did Mom do right? What did Dad do right? What would you change?
4. What memories do you have from the first time Dad was gone?
5. What are your concerns for the future?
6. What would be your best advice for another child in a similar situation?
7. Do you have anything to add?
8. How did you see God helping you through this time?

Child A: age 20

My initial reaction was, really?! Seriously, after all the jerks I have dated, all the people who have treated me wrong, all the jerks you tried to warn me about and how you lectured me about them, AND YOU DO THIS? He was my last living hope for a true gentleman. Then he did what he did. I also didn't understand how he did not think about his kids, like what was so important about that moment that he didn't think about his own flesh. It made me feel like fulfilling that sexual urge meant more to him than his own family. It also made me feel like maybe we did something wrong, like were we stressing him out so much that he caved? Now, I identify him as two people, My Dad and then, let's say, Joey. lol. Personally, I started to fall apart about eight months after; when everything settled down. I didn't want to talk about it. I didn't want to think about it. What good was it going to do me? Do I really want Mom to see me crying? Instead I picked up my life, and now when I do start to get sad, I go for a run or head to the gym. I still see no point in being upset over it. What's done is done, I can't change it, and it doesn't concern me anymore.

I can't really say that anyone helped me initially. I never opened up to anyone. I didn't really feel like talking to anyone about it; I was always afraid of sounding negative. I guess really what helped me was that I worked 11 hour shifts five days a week, so I was pretty busy. And then I added working out and eating right, so my brain went elsewhere 97% of the time. I started focusing little by little on my health and getting into shape. With my personality, I like to research, so having a "project" like learning to be healthy, kept my mind off things.

I'm not really sure where the right and wrong line went with this whole thing, because there aren't really a group of set rules for this kind of mess. What I can say, is that no one killed each other, and my dad was humbled beyond belief. I was glad that my mom told my grandparents immediately, because my grandfather made me feel VERY safe and comforted. I knew he would take care of us. What I would change though, is what I learned after everything happened. A lot of times I would sit and talk to my parents when they got in a fight, or when either of them was feeling down. I love both my parents dearly, and would do anything to help them out. I feel like in this situation, I should have simply been the child. Knowing everything, or at least a lot, after the initial news was too much for me now that I look at it.

The memories I have are more than I thought I would have. I remember Dad always being gone, that he was always on "business trips". When he did "come home" he was only home for a bit and then had to "go back to work". Obviously, I know what it means now. That explains why I am so used to him being gone for work all the time now, and why it took so long for me to develop a relationship with him.

At the time, my concerns were whether or not my parents were going to stay together. I knew that if they separated, that it would be a whole new financial ball game. I knew I could support myself if I really needed to, and I had a place to go if times got tough. I remember looking into moving out so my Mom and Dad would have one less thing to worry about if they did separate; so it would be a little bit easier on their pockets.

Now, I have different concerns for the future, but on my own part. I have zero trust for any man that enters my life. As of right now, I have no interest whatsoever in getting married, or being in a relationship for that matter. Instead, I am just focusing on me, and where I want my future to go, with or without a man in my life.

My best advice is to know it's not your fault. What's done is done, and you can only move forward. Find some time to really sit and think and grieve, eat a bucket of ice cream while watching *The Notebook*, or whatever you need! Just get out the emotions. Pick yourself up, and find something new to focus on. And remember that as much as you love Mom and Dad; try not to get into all the details. All you need to know is that it happened and it sucks, from there all the information is not yours to know. Focus on YOU.

God has kept me strong, and has made me a much better person than I was before. He has shown me that not every day was going to be good, and that you need to make the best of the good moments you have. He helped me get up off my butt and make myself happy instead of waiting for other people or other things to do it.

121

Child B: age 18

What is going to happen and why did this happen? I will be okay. I will forgive and forget. My girlfriend is helping me and I want her to. She just tries to keep my mind off of the situation. Mom and Dad are just letting me leave the room. I wouldn't change anything they are doing now. My concerns for the future are that I would have to choose who to live with. I wonder whether Dad is coming back or not. For now, I will just try to forgive and forget. Let Dad try to make up for it. I am not sure if God has helped me through this. Maybe I did not reach out to Him.

Child C: age 16

To be honest I saw it coming so I rationalized it a lot. I was sort of prepared because of what I saw in the two months before it happened. There was no love so I kept telling myself the only thing that was keeping them together was the kids. I kept thinking that once we left for college they would get a divorce but I guess that is happening a little sooner. It isn't that much different now and there is not much tension over choosing the mother over the father or the father over the mother because we are with my mother mostly anyway.

My friends and my girlfriend helped me by getting my mind off of things. One friend and I went to the gas station and just talked about what happened and bought some snacks and came to the conclusion that dads are stupid and we hope that we are never like that.

In my case mom never stopped praying for him no matter how much she hated him for what he had done. She never gave up. My dad continued to support us even though in most cases the dad doesn't do that.

I don't think I would change anything because everything happens for a reason. I remember that I didn't really want to talk to my dad. I hope that because of my experiences I don't have the mindset that it is okay to get a divorce and cheat and to stay loyal. I don't want to turn into a jerk in the future. ADVICE: Don't be affected by it too much and try to make the best of it. Don't think about it. In my scenario my dad was not around most of the time because of his job so it is not very much different. Focus on school or what you like to do so that you are not pondering on the event too much. I believe God gave me a more rational view so I wasn't grieving as much as others did. I didn't cry.

Eight years ago I only remember sitting on my bed and praying.

Child D: age 15

This wasn't like my dad. I never ever would have thought my dad would do something like this. I have never seen my dad cry in my life; I saw him standing in the kitchen crying, and unable to look me in the eyes. Mom was on the couch. Before, my dad was to me, like, the "perfect" Christian, family man. I didn't know what to think. I just cried. It was hard to believe it and I couldn't wrap my mind around it. I was just kind of numb the next day, as if it was a dream; a nightmare. I couldn't look my dad in the eyes. I didn't talk to him. I wasn't mad, but sad and confused. Today, I am okay most of the time. Life is different in some ways at home, but outside of home is normal. It's actually been fine! I'm happy. Sometimes it comes to mind, though, and I'll cry myself to sleep, but it's okay. Mom has rough days, too. And I just try to be there for her.

My boyfriend definitely helped me the next day in school. He just tried to understand and was sweet to me and tried to cheer me up when he could. My friend, Lynn's daughter, helped me too. I knew I could talk to her and I am here for her, too. My best friend helped me the most. Although she doesn't and can't understand, she will listen. It's hard though.

Mom tells me things about what's going on or how she is. I love that she is honest, because now I want to know everything. She doesn't close off about it and I like that she is comfortable to talk or vent to me.

Dad kept his distance at first when it happened, which I needed. I didn't want to talk. Then he slowly got back to himself and I liked that too. I don't really know what they've done wrong in dealing with it. Dad should have been honest.

I am afraid that something might happen again; I don't know what, but something.

My advice is to find someone to talk to, because it is hard not having someone you can rely on. Church helps so much; cry when you need to. Don't stray from God, seek Him. God blesses my family so much. There are so many things that could have been so much worse. God has given me friends who have gone through similar things and who care. He has convicted my dad's heart so much, it seems. God just comforts me.

Child E: age 14

I thought my dad was stupid to throw everything away. I still think that and also his life isn't better at all. Child D helped me. We were able to talk through what we were going through with each other. She understands how it feels and I talked with my brother and my momma.

I really don't like this question (#3) because how could mom do something wrong to cause all this? She didn't do anything. She could have broken this relationship off eight years ago and not let him come back but she didn't for us, not herself. She even let him come over more so that we didn't have go to his place as much. She did everything right. My dad did a lot of things wrong but he did let us keep the house and didn't fight over custody for our sake.

The biggest thing I remember from eight years ago was when we welcomed him home. My concerns now are for my children and whom I am going to marry. All this is in God's plan for us. ADVICE: Find someone to talk to.

Child F: age 14 *(a special account of another family in crisis)*

My initial reaction was relief because my father is an abusive alcoholic. Well, he became one in the months/years before their divorce. The first thought to go through my mind was "finally!" I am still relieved that the divorce happened now. Through that time, all of my friends helped me without even knowing it! Just hanging out with my friends having fun helped me the most.

What my mom did right was taking both kids with her in the divorce. My dad didn't do anything right except pay child support on time (as far as I know). I remember the first time my dad was gone. My parents had fought one night, and it became physical. My mom called the police and the police decided to send one of them out of the house for a week so things could cool down. It was decided that my brother and I would stay with my mom, and the police asked my mother to find somewhere to stay for a week (and bring us along). We stayed in a studio apartment in a friend's backyard.

I guess the most concerning thing about the future would be if my father will continue to pay child support without any problems. ADVICE: Do not blame yourself; it is not your fault. "The Lord your God goes with you; He will never leave you nor forsake you." (Deuteronomy 31:6b)

God absolutely has everything to do with it!

"The Lord is a refuge for the oppressed, a stronghold in times of trouble." (Psalm 9:9).

Child G: age 13

I was shocked. I was devastated, upset, and mad. How could he have done that? It affected me then, but now I don't have too many emotions about it. My friends really helped me through this. I talked to them.

I don't know what Mom did right. She did everything right, but there really is no right or wrong in how she handled it. I don't know how even Dad could have handled it. Mom sometimes uses this to get more things for the house and stuff. I don't like that. Dad is doing his best to do everything for Mom. He is really trying and obeying Mom, bringing home flowers occasionally, and all that.

My worries for the future are that his work will over hear about it and Dad will get fired.

125

ADVICE: Pray to God; tell Him how you feel. Tell the Dad how you feel and then get away from him. Go do something that you do when you are mad that comforts you. Whenever I am really mad I usually go upstairs and play a video game. I can drive virtually really fast and spend all my money, and there is no danger.

I just feel like the family will never be the same. Mom is always working now, and I don't think that helps. It has definitely affected my brother and the way he acts, the respect he gives them both. My sister is really uptight and my other sister actually seems to be better. We seem to be shorter on money. Dad hasn't done much to win the boys back; we just do what he wants to do rather than hearing us. It is a guy thing. It is hard for me to follow in his ways 'cause that is kind of hard now. He always wanted me to be like him. I was mad that I didn't know all this. Dad thinks we are just . . . cool. I just look at him and think, what the heck!

I really don't see how God has helped me. I am trying to be a good person and stop my bad habits and He keeps throwing bad stuff my way. I really am trying, but it is really hard. I think God is trying to teach me a lesson, but I am trying. It is kind of a curse because after this I started getting bad grades and other bad things like losing friends and stuff. Mom has been more uptight. Teachers seem stricter. Everything is falling apart.

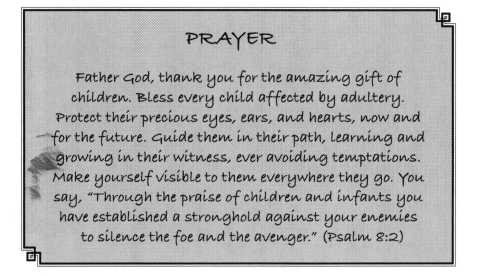

PRAYER

Father God, thank you for the amazing gift of children. Bless every child affected by adultery. Protect their precious eyes, ears, and hearts, now and for the future. Guide them in their path, learning and growing in their witness, ever avoiding temptations. Make yourself visible to them everywhere they go. You say, "Through the praise of children and infants you have established a stronghold against your enemies to silence the foe and the avenger." (Psalm 8:2)

Let us praise you daily for your power and goodness.
Continue to allow me to be a blessing and an
example in their lives and not a hindrance. AMEN

POWER

"And when you and your children return to the
Lord your God and obey him with all your heart
and with all your soul according to everything I
command you today, then the Lord your God will
restore your fortunes and have compassion on
you and gather you again from all the nations
where he scattered you." (Deut. 30:2-3)

"Come, my children, listen to me; I will teach
you the fear of the Lord." (Psalm 34:11)

"Jesus said, 'Let the little children come to me, and
do not hinder them, for the kingdom of heaven
belongs to such as these'." (Matthew 19:14)

"Do you hear what these children are saying?" they
asked him. "Yes," replied Jesus, "have you never read,
"'from the lips of children and infants you, Lord,
have called forth your praise'?" (Matthew 21:16)

Scripture Suggestions

PSALM 145

I will exalt you, my God the King;
I will praise your name for ever and ever.
Every day I will praise you
and extol your name for ever and ever.
Great is the Lord and most worthy of praise;
his greatness no one can fathom.
One generation will commend your works to another;
they will tell of your mighty acts.
They will speak of the glorious splendor of your majesty,
and I will meditate on your wonderful works.
They will tell of the power of your awesome works,
and I will proclaim your great deeds.
They will celebrate your abundant goodness
and joyfully sing of your righteousness.
The Lord is gracious and compassionate,
slow to anger and rich in love.
The Lord is good to all;
he has compassion on all he has made.
All you have made will praise you, O Lord;
your saints will extol you.
They will tell of the glory of your kingdom
and speak of your might,
so that all men may know of your mighty acts
and the glorious splendor of your kingdom
Your kingdom is an everlasting kingdom, and your
dominion endures through all generations.

The Lord is faithful to all his promises
And loving toward all he has made.
The Lord upholds all those who fall
and lifts up all who are bowed down.
The eyes of all look to you,
and you give them their food at the proper time.
You open your hand
and satisfy the desires of every living thing.
The Lord is righteous in all his ways
and loving toward all he has made.
The Lord is near to all who call on him,
to all who call on him in truth.
He fulfills the desires of those who fear him;
he hears their cry and saves them.
The Lord watches over all who love him,
but all the wicked he will destroy.
My mouth will speak in praise of the Lord.
Let every creature praise his holy name
For ever and ever."

"Therefore we do not lose heart. Though outwardly we are wasting away, yet inwardly we are being renewed day by day. For our light and momentary troubles are achieving for us an eternal glory that far outweighs them all. So we fix our eyes not on what is seen, but on what is unseen, since what is seen is temporary, but what is unseen is eternal." (1 Corinthians 4:16-18)

Suggested Reading

1. ANY version of the Bible. We used the *New International Version*
2. *How to Save Your Marriage Alone* by Ed Wheat, M.D.
3. *Power of a Praying Wife* by Stormie Omartian
4. *The Meaning of Marriage* by Timothy Keller
5. *After the Affair* by Janis Abrahms Spring, PH.D. with Michael Spring
6. *Love is a Choice* by Gary Smalley
7. *From the Father's Heart* by Charles Slagle
8. *Answers to Life's Difficult Questions* by Rick Warren
9. *The Lady, Her Lover and Her Lord* by T.D. Jakes
10. *The Rose Garden and the Ring* by Lynn & Christine

Suggested Playlist

1. "Stand" by Susan Ashton
2. "Overcome" by Mandisa
3. "Sometimes He Calms The Storm" by Scott Krippayne
4. "Jesus, What A Beautiful Name" by Darlene Zschech
5. "Love Song 4 a Savior" by Jars of Clay
6. "Mercy Came Running" by Phillips, Craig & Dean
7. "Agnus Dei" by Michael W. Smith
8. "Jehovah" by Amy Grant
9. "I Will Not Be Moved" by Natalie Grant
10. "Shackles" by Mary Mary
11. "Mercy Seat" by Vicki Yohe
12. "Praise You In this Storm" by Casting Crowns
13. "Peace Be Still" by Al Denson
14. "Be the One" by Al Denson
15. "I Can Only Imagine" by MercyMe
16. "Good Life" by One Republic
17. "In The Light" by DC Talk

Works Cited

Omartian, S. (1997). *The Power of a Praying Wife*. Oregon: Harvest House Publishers.

Wheat, E. (1983). *how to save your marriage alone*. Michigan: Zondervan

Forgive. (n.d.). Retrieved from 1.http://www.merriam-webster.com/dictionary/

(n.d.). Retrieved from http://quotationsbook.com/quote/47877/

Dr. Reed, John W. Retrieved from http://www.marriagehealing.org/hosea.php

(n.d.). Retrieved from http://www.openbible.info/topics/what_goes_around_comes_around

Columbidae. (n.d.). Retrieved from www.wikipedia.org

Cut and Paste Prayers

At the suggestion of our initial readers, we have included this additional section for you. The left side of the page has a larger margin so that you are able to easily cut out these pages. Place them in your Bible, on your desk, on your walls and mirrors, in your car; wherever you need help to pray. We hope they will help draw you into a deeper prayer life and encourage you!

—Lynn and Christine

PRAYER—How Big Is Your Faith?

LORD I AM OVERWHELMED!!! I am confused and I am hurt. I cry out to you in agony! I know you will never leave me or forsake me but I feel so alone. Draw near to me and hold me in your arms. Comfort and guide me. I know my heart longs to do whatever you would have for me. Teach me to be open to your word and hear the still small voice of the Holy Spirit amidst the loudness of my confused and desperate thoughts. Make my will your will. I need your guidance more than ever. Forgive me for the thoughts in my head and the anger in my heart. Help me not to sin in my anger. I love you Lord and I want to follow the path you have set for me because I believe in your promises. AMEN

PRAYER—Walking With God

El Sali, God my Rock, Help me to remember to be in fervent prayer so I can hear you clearly. Teach me to recognize your voice. Help me to be still and quiet in your presence so that I do not miss a single word from you. Be my rock to lean on, to take a stand in your name, and to lift me closer to you so I can feel your presence. Walk with me through the darkness and light my path. Bathe with me in the sunlight of your victories! Holy Spirit, remind me to continue the walk and pray without ceasing. Help me to pray for (spouse's name) so that his eyes are open to your truths even when I do not feel like praying for him. Let the thin thread that I am hanging on be woven into double braided rope, strengthened by your grace and mercy. Forgive me when my thoughts stray and when I feel like I cannot find you, for I know you are there, always. AMEN

PRAYER—Immediate Assistance

Lord Creator, you made me in my mother's womb. You know exactly who I am. I submit myself to you daily. I give (spouse's name) to you as well. I fight feelings of sadness, loneliness, frustration and loss. I am lost . . . but know that you will help me. I am human in all of my strengths and frailties. Holy Spirit, order my thoughts and guide me in the paths of righteousness. AMEN

PRAYER—Tools and Weapons

Lord! As hard as I try to keep order and peace in my home I feel like I'm just a train wreck! And the more I discover details about my spouse's deception, the more pain I feel in my heart even though I long for the truth. Holy Spirit, help me to use the resources that you bless me with and open my eyes and heart to your healing. I understand that I will probably not be rescued from the feelings of anguish but I'm pleading with you to point me toward the truth of the Bible and things you place in my life for comfort until this storm subsides and your glory is made known. Thank you for being my omnipresent (everywhere at all times), omniscient (all-knowing), and omnipotent (all-powerful) God. AMEN

PRAYER—Loss Of Control

Psalm 23

"The Lord is my shepherd; I shall not be in want.
He makes me lie down in green pastures,
he leads me beside still waters,
he restores my soul
He guides me in paths of righteousness
for his name's sake.
Even though I walk
through the valley of the shadow of death,
I will fear no evil,
for you are with me;
your rod and your staff,
they comfort me.
You prepare a table before me
in the presence of my enemies.
You anoint my head with oil;
my cup overflows.
Surely goodness and love will follow me
all the days of my life,
and I will dwell in the house of the Lord
forever." Amen

PRAYER—Emotions/Rollercoaster

Elohe Mauzi, God our Strength, teach me to be humble in my speech and actions even though it doesn't seem fair that I am the one who needs to be humbled. Your word says "that you guide the humble in what is right and teach them your way." (Psalm 25:9) And you "crown the humble with victory." (Psalm 149:4) I release control of my future completely to you so that together we may be victorious and can shout to the world of your glory and goodness! Through my ups and downs help me to be respectful to those around me, keeping my emotions from affecting others. I love you Lord. AMEN

PRAYER—Marriage/Divorce

LORD, Creator, your word says in Matthew 19:6, "so they are no longer two but one. Therefore what God has joined together, let man not separate." I know how you feel about marriage and divorce. I know you have a perfect plan. Give me the strength, courage, and insight to follow your plan your way. However things may turn out in the end I know that you are with me and have my best interests in mind. Please keep me safe from the lies that Satan wants me to hear. I put my hope and my trust in you. AMEN

PRAYER—Grass Not Greener

Jehovah-Jireh, my Provider, teach me patience and understanding. Help me to wait for you. I am tired and I feel like the decisions I have to make are unfair. I know that you are patient with me and do not want "anyone to perish, but everyone to come to repentance." (2 Peter 3:9) I want to feel your peace so that I can stay out of your way in order to hear your voice clearly. Thank you for your constant presence in my life! AMEN

PRAYER—Sweet Children

Jehovah Raah, the Lord my Shepherd, you are the good shepherd. You laid down your life for the sheep of your pasture. You protect us from the wolf. You know me inside and out as I know you know my children inside and out. Lord guard my precious children's eyes, ears, and hearts from worry, pain, and negative influences. Guide me in caring for their needs. I lay my children at your feet. AMEN

PRAYER—Revenge

El Nathan Neqamah, God who executes vengeance, you are my hiding place, my refuge, and my strong tower. I know that I do not need to take revenge into my own hands. Your justice and subsequent consequences of my spouse's betrayals and choices reach far beyond my meager earthly view. I want to be filled with good thoughts and actions and not with the bitterness of revenge and hatred. Please show (spouse) that his hiding place, refuge and strong tower are in you and not in what the world offers. Thank you for letting me express my thoughts, good and bad, to you in prayer. Lead me on the path of righteousness. AMEN

PRAYER—God's Blessings

Yah Weh Nissi, the Lord is my Banner; open my eyes to see your blessings! I long to hold on to your word. Go before me declaring victory in your name over the struggles I encounter in my walk. Thank you for your acts of encouragement along the way. Thank you in advance for the work you are doing in my life and in my spouse's life . . . never failing to recognize our needs. Show favor to my spouse when he makes good choices. Allow him to feel victory in the moment of obedience and to feel your glory. AMEN

149

PRAYER—Adulteress

Elohay Mishpat, God of justice, I am finding it very difficult to pray. On my own it is impossible for me to understand and forgive. In time, teach me how to forgive her and my spouse for the pain they have caused me, my family and my friends. I thank you for your promises made clear in your Word. And as much as I am able, I give the adulteress to you; I trust you. Keep me from taking it upon myself to handle. Restore me as a child of God, not a person of this world. AMEN

PRAYER—God's Promises

El-elyon, the most high God, I praise you for your word, instruction, and blessings. Your promises encourage me to move through and beyond my current struggles. I ask you to continue to remind me to turn to your word when I fall. Use me and bless me!
Amen

PRAYER—For Spouse

Johovah Ori, the Lord my Light, I intercede in prayer for my spouse and the temptations he faces. I pray that you open his eyes to see the light of your truths and ward off the evil of this world. Make him deaf to the negative influences and attune to your words and your way so that he is able to rise above. Take captive of his heart and cause him to be a man after your spirit. Lord if he says "Hear my voice when I call Oh Lord; be merciful to me (Psalm 27:7) I know you will be there to answer his plea. Let his pride be in his wife and children, his walk to be toward you, his sleep to be instructional (Psalm 16:7), and his awake time to be fully aware of your plans for him. AMEN

PRAYER—The Final Days

Lord, please deliver my spouse from his past. Help him to clearly see his mistakes and release him so he does not live in them but learn from them. Help him to break free and move into the future you have for him. Deliver him from temptations and touch his heart. Give him eyes to see you clearly and ears to hear your word. Shower him with people, places and things in his life that remind him of you. I pray for his salvation! Fill him with your spirit and flush out all that is evil. Help him to shut out the negative influences. Convict him of all his sins so there may not be anything hidden that has power over him. Remind him that you make all things new. Renew his mind. Let him know of your love through me, his children and the good influences you have placed in his life. I put my trust in you. AMEN

PRAYER—The Rose Garden and the Ring

Jehovah Goelekh, the Lord thy Redeemer, I am amazed by your vision and your plan for my life. There was no way I could have ever imagined how you would weave together events over time to arrive at the point where I am today. I can't comprehend how you can put together everything to your glory, my benefit and even to my spouse's benefit but am very glad you do! You see all the details, the big picture, when I can't. Your ways are perfect and I hope to never doubt your concern for me in this big world. Thank you for your faithfulness and redemption and help me to continue to seek you in all things. Please bless me and my family on this new journey. AMEN

PRAYER—Forgiveness

El-nose, a forgiving God, help me to find forgiveness in this unforgiving world. Forgive me for my unclean thoughts, anger, and doubt. I release my emotions to you . . . by your will and not my own. You forgive us for our sins instantly because we are your children and you are a just God. You are perfect but we are not. I know that not forgiving someone hurts me more. I long for the relief that comes with true forgiveness. Teach me your way. AMEN

PRAYER—Repercussions/Trust

Elohim Lacham, God who fights for me, I acknowledge that these struggles I face are a battle for my soul. I belong to you! There are many obstacles that my spouse and I face daily. I know these obstacles can break us down or be used for your glory. Help us to draw on your strength and focus on the bigger picture for our future instead of dwelling on the past. Lord, I need you to take control of my thoughts and to tame my tongue so that I am able to heal. Please turn all the lies into truths so that trust can be re-established. Help this fight to not be with myself but standing with you against Satan and his attempts to tear me down! AMEN

PRAYER—Miracles

Gelah Raz, a revealer of mysteries, WOW!!!Thank you for your miracles, small and big. Help us to remember that if our faith is big then we will ask for big things and watch you move mountains. Your glory continues to amaze me! No matter how long I have on this earth, I know that I will want to spend it with you. In you are my hope, my peace, and my comfort. AMEN

PRAYER—Updates

Yasha, my Savior, from this day forward, we vow to stand together and keep looking toward the heavens for direction in all that we do. It is our desire to encourage others in strength and righteousness through our struggles and when we fall into doubt and despair, help us to support one another and redirect our paths. Take all our "gifts" and failures and use them to your glory. Help others to relate to and learn from our choices, good and bad. Lord, you know I am not perfect. Thank you for your sacrifice and unfailing love! "Praise be to the Lord, to God our Savior, who daily bears our burdens." (Psalm 68:19) AMEN

PRAYER—Your Witness

Cameke Nephesh, Sustainer of my soul, you are always here for me! Thank you for the people you have placed in my life that encourage me. Remind me to be a light to someone else and to use my story as a witness. I realize that I'm not 'whole' yet but give me the strength to reach out where you would have me. Day by day Lord . . . with you. AMEN

PRAYER—A Parting Word

El Shaddai, God who meets our needs, I will wait on you. Your word says, "Indeed the very hairs of your head are all numbered. Do not be afraid." (Luke 12:7) Thank you for knowing me inside and out and loving me regardless. Bless my family and my home. In your name, AMEN

PRAYER—From the Mouths of Babes

Father God, thank you for the amazing gift of children. Bless every child affected by adultery. Protect their precious eyes, ears, and hearts, now and for the future. Guide them in their path, learning and growing in their witness, ever avoiding temptations. Make yourself visible to them everywhere they go. You say, "Through the praise of children and infants you have established a stronghold against your enemies to silence the foe and the avenger." (Psalm 8:2) Let us praise you daily for your power and goodness. Continue to allow me to be a blessing and an example in their lives and not a hindrance. AMEN

About the Authors

Lynn—Wife, Mother, Domestic Goddess, Military Veteran, Property Manager, Student and most importantly Christian. Lynn's faith has been tested time and time again but nothing has compared to surviving the affair of a spouse. No doubt the effects of adultery no one should have to endure but with God you can come through not only a better person but stronger in faith and living a more fulfilled life! Lynn continues to live, work, and grow in Christ with her two children and golden retriever.

———⁓∿◦◦◦◦∿⁓———

Christine—Wife, Mother, Domestic Goddess, Vocalist, Seamstress, Baker, and most importantly Christian. Christine has endured the ravaging effects of her spouse's betrayal. This life altering experience should never be a part of a person's testimony but is rampant in today's culture. While unfortunate, she is able to use her testimony for God's glory. Christine, her husband, four children, and three dogs reside, work, and grow in Christ.

Check it out...
Faith in the Midst
Study Guide
by: Lynn and Christine

The **Faith in the Midst Study Guide** takes it one step further and applies the concepts set forth in the book, to a bible study format. The guide was designed to be used in conjunction with the book, however, is not limited to the topic of adultery alone. Here is a glimpse of what is covered inside:

- How big is your faith?
- Daily walking with God through crisis.
- Options for help.
- How to deal with out of control feelings and thoughts.
- Is the grass always greener?
- Children and adversity.
- Revenge and Forgiveness.
- God's Promises.
- Time and Miracles.

The bible is a living word that takes us from despair to hope and understanding if we rely on God to pull us all the way through. Set aside time to go on a journey toward healing or join a group and share!

Keep Connected...

Feel free to contact us through our Facebook page:
https://www.facebook.com/pages/
The-Rose-Garden-and-the-Ring/519131274831633?fref=ts

Printed in the United States
By Bookmasters